ECHOES FROM THE PAST:
INTERPRETING ZIMBABWE'S
DECORATIVE SYMBOLS

Pathisa Nyathi and Kudzai Chikomo

ECHOES FROM THE PAST:
INTERPRETING ZIMBABWE'S
DECORATIVE SYMBOLS

ISBN 978 0 7974 5014 1

EAN 978 0 7974 5014 1

Copyright © Pathisa Nyathi & Kudzai Chikomo

Published by Amagugu Publishers

Published in 2016

Contents

Preface

The sun's bright rays of hope light up the eastern sky. The pitch black blanket of prejudice, self-centredness and arrogance recedes ahead of advancing day. It is time for rebirth, re-awakening, revival, regeneration and reassertion by the sleeping giant. Africa is beginning to tell her own story. Echoes from Source reverberate through the dark valleys of her story distorted and mutilated.

The cradle of humanity is the cradle of human wisdom and knowledge. The continent is beginning to shirk off shackles of domination, of cosmological imperialism and epistemological arrogance. A television programme that I am watching strikes me as showcasing African decorative symbols and earth colours. It is a Nigerian programme whose set is completely dominated by enchanting, charming and delightful circles, chevrons, waves, curves, triangles and spirals. The presenter, an immaculately kitted out lady, is resplendent with enthralling symbols of triangles and curvy lines. The earth colours, inspired by Mother Earth, a recurring theme in African Thought, complement the artistic symbols. How could she escape our language of symbolism and metaphor?

I see an immense river, Mulonga, *mulonga mupati,* rise from a distant Source, swiftly snaking her way forward. In his lustful journey, he engages Mother Earth in an erotic embrace that gives birth to life, her progeny. This is another enduring African theme involving God Nyaminyami of the BaTonga. The river is a symbol, so is Mother Earth. Both are reality in addition to being symbols of a deeper meaning. Through symbols, designed by our

Kasambabezi (Zambezi River)

minds and given life by our hands, we allow our minds to be inspired by environments near and far, terrestrial and cosmic. We tell enduring stories from ancestral Source to present and future generations. Who muffled echoes from Source? Who mutilated our symbols and altered messages that they carried? Who chose to become our spokesperson when we have our mouths? Let echoes of our symbols, pregnant with messages from Source, of Mulonga and Mother Earth eternally entangled in symbolic embrace, reverberate down the valleys of time.

Nyaminyami Sculpture at Lake Kariba

Mulonga reconnects us, distance spanned by her length, a continuing band surging with boundless erotic zeal. Mother Earth, smiling wide open, reminds us of our created destiny; their embrace, our hope, carried by the shining sun's rays of optimism and resurgence. Do I hear the sounds of African drums, of ululating mothers, of an ecstatic environment released, liberated and finally respected and honoured; joys of equilibrium, of balance re-established, our philosophy triumphal? This is eternity as created and understood by Source, of a community eternally regenerating. Have we not immortalized continuity through our symbols? Have we not seen individuals perish and humanity enduring? This is our story as narrated by Source and handed down, understood, misunderstood and sometimes demonized. Morning is the beginning of life, chasing away night, nay of death. Death retreats ahead of life. So does night ahead of light. Life is born of death, a strange couple engaged in a fatally infinite embrace, together in sequence: birth, growth, development, degeneration, decay, death and rebirth, ad infinitum. This is what our minds learnt from Mind at Source. Our symbols are pregnant with offspring from Source. Muffled and confused sounds are not sounds from Source.

Cemeteries of death are cemeteries of life; of death and resurrection, of eternity, immortality, perpetuity, infinity, endlessness and imperishability. Our decorative symbols are our language of expression, dependable emissaries from Source, *Mulonga mupati*, into the warm moist depths of life-giving Mother Earth. Our struggles of betrayal, of Mbuya Nehanda conveniently forgotten, of Source derided and abused, of echoes muffled and smothered, loom large. Day swallows night. Our memories rekindle and reconnect. We rejoice when Africa slithers like a snake caressed into life, a life infused with meaning, of ancient wisdom entombed in symbols on baskets, mats, headrests, wooden plates, ivory diagnostic bones and clay pots. Cemetery consumed our forgetfulness and yet gives us lasting memory, a joyous reconnection and enduring bond with Source.

What frail and fragile moth, what elegant exquisite butterfly, shall drink of my flower's nectar and have audacity and temerity to silt and suffocate *Mulonga mupati* and dry Source and see morning? Only Source, brightly lit by morning rays, holds hope to light up Source and reveal *Mulonga mupati*, with darkness folded, and sharpens our minds and wits to see Mulonga's impregnating erotic entangle and fertile embrace of obliging Mother Earth. Allow Africa to speak and teach her offspring!

Introduction

Our art was expressed through our material culture. "It reflected the African world through images. It was part of an African people's awareness of their world. It expressed their beliefs, customs, values and lifestyle. As a mode of communication, it was oral, graphic, visual, three-dimensional and symbolic. Art was integrated into technology as part of craftsmanship. Craftsmanship and aesthetics combined in the material culture. Functionality and beauty fused into one skill. Art was thus not only utilitarian. The order and symmetry that is evident in the art was an expression of a desire for a well-organized and beautiful life. The art was basically naturalist as it reflected the objects that existed in the artists' environment. It also enhanced the status of the owner (Chiwome 1996: 96).

A people's worldview and cosmology are a result of the interaction between nature and culture. Africans observed nature and got inspired by it. Certain natural attributes in particular appealed to Africans. The seasons of the year were repetitive, cyclical and characterized by birth, death and rebirth. Summer is symbolic of life; however it is not a permanent phenomenon. Autumn follows and life wanes and declines. Winter follows autumn and is symbolic and an approximation of death, a period of total rest in readiness for the next lively stage. Winter is the time when vegetation takes a rest, sheds its leaves (in tropical regions at least). Vigorous and sustained exercise comes after a period of rest characterized by minimum utilisation of energy.

Spring is a part of the cycle that holds promise for a new life. Trees develop buds and flowers blossom. This is the time when trees begin the all-important process of developing seeds, which give life to new trees-this is the continuity of a species. For the Africans this marks the beginning of a new year-a nature-determined period that lies behind the process of fertility, continuity, perpetuity, immortality, endlessness and infinity. Summer is followed by autumn, and the cycle is repeated indefinitely. It is this inherent cyclical birth-death-rebirth that lies behind eternal life. Perpetual life or continuity is assured through this 'circle of life.' The

Blooming Jacaranda trees in spring

African learnt something and sought to imitate such a natural phenomenon which carries the desired trait of continuity. The vital question is what causes the cyclical seasons that translate to regeneration or renewal which lies at the root of continuity?

Leafless Jacarandas in winter

The diurnal cycle equally conveys the same idea of continuity through regeneration and renewal. The sun rises in the morning, a phenomenon that is equivalent to the onset of spring and summer-a period of life and growth. The sun gives life to both flora and fauna on which humans and animals alike are dependent. However, if the sun perpetuated, i.e. did not set, life on Earth would be obliterated by the scorching heat. In order to perpetuate life, the sun sets and night falls. Temperatures drop. Night, the absence of the sun, is equivalent to death. If the sun did not rise in the morning, life would be doomed. The African observed the cyclical alternation between day and night as a source of continued life. The diurnal cycle is behind the perpetuation of life, a sought after attribute.

The moon is the most visible of the heavenly bodies at night. Its movement or change is observed to symbolize continuity. A new moon that is observed in the western sky was monitored closely by Africans. For example, among the BaRozvi of Zimbabwe royalty lived at the highest point of the hill or mountain. Their political and socio-economic status was symbolized through physical height.

"Bohhe bagele dombo,
BoTjibumba bagele dombo,
BoNthoyiwa bagele dombo,
Zwilanda zwigele pasi pasi kuBambanalo,
Heyo mbila mudombo-ntombo,
Muyilobe neswimbo(Nyathi 2014: 17).

8

Rulers lived on mountains. Lower class people inhabited lower ground, on Bambanalo Hill. This was given in reference to the occupation of Mapungubgwe Hill which is located between the Limpopo and Shashe rivers. Mapungubgwe, the hill of jackals, is higher that Bambanalo an adjacent but lower hill. A device known as *'ziso'* in Tjilozwi or Tjikalanga was maintained to monitor the movement of the moon. The mask-like device was placed on the face to view the new moon on the western sky. The device also had a small depression into which water was added for washing the gazer's face. Finally, there was a place where incense was burnt to symbolically cleanse the darkness associated with the 'death' of the moon.

Among the Ndebele when the new moon appeared the people gazed the moon and shouted, *"Kholiwe hamba lomkhuhlane!"* New moon, take away the disease. Among the Bakalanga a children's poem was recited in recognition of the new moon.

> *Howa mwedzi wagala,*
> *Wagala panahhunduntule,*
> *Hhunduntule wati kama n'ombe,*
> *Kama n'ombe tinde kaTjatilisa,*
> *KaTjatilisa kuna mhulutjatja,*
> *Mhulutjatja dzinotambatamba,*
> *Tambatamba nezwanana zwadzo.*

> *Hokwana inamabala,*
> *Mabala anonga ejeletjele,*
> *Jeletjele haya pogala,*
> *Pagala panazwibululu,*
> *Zwibululu nhungulu dzayibva,*
> *Dzayibva pampanga ntshwa,*
> *Mpanga ntshwa waBaabelenga,*
> *Baabelenga bakatshwa milomo,*
> *Bakatshwa milomo nematama mafo,*
> *Matama mafo,*
> *Matama mafo asingabhayike,*
> *Anobhayika unatjitje,*
> *No unaujuju ijakabvu buloyi,*

9

Mbudzi dzakaTembo,
Dzakapelela mutjidziba ngelele,
Wuntshi poro!
(Saul Gwakuba Ndlovu, Harrisvale, 03/ 02/ 2016)

Essentially, the poem celebrated the emergence of the new moon as signaling a safer period free of witches. The belief was that witches roamed around and carried out their nefarious activities when there was no moon that lit the night. There is some comparison between what the Ndebele and the Bakalanga believed. The new moon heralded better life.

The moon has the attribute of growing after its birth. This it does by waxing till it is a full moon. Here the moon symbolizes complete life and the highest prospects for successful cultural activities. After full moon, the moon begins to wane till it 'dies.' Once again, there is birth, growth, development, degeneration, decay, death and rebirth or cyclical regeneration or renewal. The 'lunar cycle' imparts the idea of continuity through rebirth and regeneration and inevitably inspired the nature and timing of cultural activities.

The human cycle also followed a cycle. A baby is born, grows, develops, gets old and degenerates and dies. At death the spirit exits the corpse and comes back to inhabit a living being. All the cited cases illustrate the expression of continuity in nature, in particular the changes initiated by cosmic bodies. The cosmos is seen as being infinite-with no beginning and no end. The cosmos was thus imitated in terms of its inherent ability to regenerate itself or to live forever. If one were to pinpoint one cosmic trait that Africans sought to imitate it would be the idea of continuity, infinity, fertility, imperishability, immortality, endlessness and perpetuity.

The question then is how did the Africans replicate the cosmic attribute in their cultural lives? They achieved this in more ways than one. Their rituals and ceremonies did express the idea of continuity. This has been ably demonstrated during the installation of chiefs among the Shona (Chigwedere 2014). The installation of a VaPfumbi chief is a good example. The deceased chief's body was closely guarded by

relatives till it decayed completely. The aim was to retrieve a stone that the chief swallowed when he was chosen chief. The stone stayed in his stomach all the time till his demise. The stone was, in the first instance, obtained from the stomach of a crocodile. The VaPfumbi are of the crocodile totem, Ngwenya/Ngwena. The key consideration is the crocodile and its important attribute rendered to it by virtue of its body shape. The crocodile is a "chevron animal" just like its cousins in the reptile group. The stone, by virtue of its having stayed within the stomach of a crocodile, had the attribute of infinity or continuity infused into or imparted onto it. The attribute of continuity which is expressed by the chevron symbol will be illustrated later in this book. Once the stone is retrieved it is administered to all chieftainship claimants. The one who qualifies manages to swallow the stone and retains it within his stomach till his own death. The chieftainship lineage is maintained, consolidated and continued into the future, thus the idea of continuity is fulfilled and expressed.

Among the Shona several items of royalty were presented to the new chief: elephant foot stool, leopard skin, lion skin, ceremonial axe(gano), sword(bakatwa(and the conus shell, (ndoro).The various items were passed down the lineage in a lateral line, that is from chief to his brothers in the other 'houses'(Chigwedere 2014; Ellert 2002). The conus shell with its spiraling shape, symbolises perpetuity and continuity. The chosen was bound on to embracing the attribute of eternity. Theoretically the spiral goes on and on ad infinitum.

The various crafts in Africa's material culture also carried the idea of continuity as inspired by the cosmos. Their design is characterized by circularity. The baskets are circular, so are the clay pots. In fact, the artifacts do not have right angles. African design was thus characterized by the circular design which was captured in architecture, designs of cattle byres, stone-walled settlements; military formation innovated by King Tshaka (the chest-horn formation). Cosmic bodies including their orbits are circular or elliptical.

Visual arts are cultural expressions. They are informed and guided by a people's cosmology, worldview, philosophy and beliefs. In fact, cultural practices emanate from their cosmological underpinnings. The decorative symbols, while expressing aesthetics, also do carry important meanings or messages concerning ideas people have about the environment, both terrestrial and cosmic. However, for Africa, these symbols, being a fossilized art form, came riding on the surfaces of functional or utility objects such as clay pots, ilala baskets, snuff boxes, ceremonial axes(*makano*), walking sticks, headrests, wooden plates, wooden stools, glass beadwork, sleeping and sitting reed mats, Zimbabwe birds, stone walls in Zimbabwe type settlements, leather aprons, spears, scabbards(*mapakatwa*), inter alia.

Performances are no exception. Singers and dancers form a circle when performing: those ululating, singing and clapping hands. "Do not break the circle," Africans will say. The dancers execute circular motion (Nyathi and Chikomo 2012; Nyathi and Chikomo 2013). The same idea of continuity is captured in their languages. The Ndebele of Zimbabwe and the Zulu of South Africa say, *"Ukuzala yikuzelula."* To give birth to children is to add to oneself (Stewart 2005). The two peoples also say, *"Ukwanda kwaliwa ngumthakathi."* Witches are not amused when they see people increasing in population. The word '*ukwanda*' captures the idea of multiplication which is the concept of continuity; increasing in population and extending into the future and occupying more territory. A Xhosa expression also carries the idea of continuity, especially through renewal and regeneration as captured in lunar cycles. *"Umafa avuke njengenyanga."* It dies and rises like the moon (Stewart 2005). The Ovambo of Namibia say, *"Aakulu siluka aape taa tumbu."* The old go down and the young arise.

What is critically important though is to note that different African peoples embraced the all-important concept of continuity (Mbiti 1969). They do so in different ways just as shown above. Their rituals /ceremonies, crafts, performances, designs, languages (e.g. proverbs), folklore and songs all carry the message of eternity, continuity, perpetuity, infinity, fertility, imperishability, endlessness and immortality. In fact, it goes beyond this. Their medical and health traditions seek to maintain the body in a healthy state till one is biologically mature to participate in the natural process that ensures and guarantees continuity-i.e., sexual reproduction. Their rain making ceremonies and rituals seek to make sure rains fall so that food is produced, which food sustains life. When they fortify their villages, huts and themselves, they are, in actual fact, countering the machinations of witches who would otherwise seek to bewitch and kill them, thus in the process negating the idea of continuity. One can go on and on and what will become apparent is that a lot of energy, time, innovation and technology went towards ensuring continuity of families, lineages and communities. This book however, focuses on the visual arts, in particular the decorative symbols of the various ethnic groups in Zimbabwe, as expressions of the idea of continuity.

Chapter 1
ART FOR COMMUNICATION

Art communicates effortlessly. There are messages that are encoded into artwork. Encoding is done by the artist. The consumer decodes the messages in order to fully appreciate the inherent or underlying meanings. "The human mind is looking for meanings and giving attributes to things. This is a part of the process to make sense of life. It shows our longing for belonging (Kerber 2015:58). Art is expressive culture. Through creativity, a people's culture is expressed and articulated. It is possible to work from a people's art and discern their culture and cosmology.

There are critical aspects of culture that are captured through visual expressions. Cosmology, which embraces the nature of beingness, ontology and mythology, is one such. We thus expect, in African visual art expressions, to find African ideas relating to the group and the individual. According to African Thought, a man is defined in reference to his community, not by any of his physical or psychological characteristics. It is only by "rootedness" in one's community that one may come to be known as a man. Language and social rules bind people with other community members and ancestors. In the African view it is the community which defines the person as a person, not some isolated static of rationality, will or meaning (Ifeanya A Menkiti).

This universal African philosophy is expressed, as part of "*ubuntu*", "*botho*", "*hunhu*" social philosophy among the Sotho and Nguni peoples of southern Africa: "*Motho ke motho ka batho*", "*Umuntu ngumuntu ngabantu.*" The idea is indeed expressed through the ubiquitous circular design as expressed through architecture, village layout, design of cattle byres, and design of various artifacts. The circle communicates the idea of community solidarity and communication. The community's priority over the individual is inherent in circular designs as found in clay pots and baskets. Pottery design communicates well before considerations of embellishment. The designs themselves are codes of communication generated within a culture. When alterations to the designs of African crafts are made there is regrettable loss of messages and meanings that were handed down the generations. Such vital African heritage is sacrificed on the altar of market forces. Western consumers come with their design preferences which, through the use of buying power, lead to the abandonment of African designs that were infused with meanings, in particular relating to the people's cosmology, aesthetics and axiology.

This is regretted all the more considering that the African craftsperson had not, in the least, appreciated the meanings resident in the designs and the art carried by the objects of utility. The messages and meanings reside both in design and also in the art carried on the surfaces of utility objects. The two reinforce each other. Generally, artifacts carry circular designs on which art, which also carries circular designs, is executed. Both are informed by the same cosmology and that explains why the created designs carry or convey the same meaning. As shall be explained later, there is in reality, one dominant design that is configured in numerous ways thus resulting in seemingly different decorative symbols. We argue that the decorative symbols were artistic renditions at the time when they were first created in the mind and executed on utility and ceremonial objects. Ceremonial objects should be viewed as utility objects. Principles that characterize art equally apply to Africa's decorative symbols: unity, the sense of oneness, of coherence: balance-the equitable distribution of lightness, heaviness of colour, texture, forms and empty spaces. Another important principle is rhythm-the repetition of art elements to lend to the eye across the whole picture plane (Pashapa 2009).

The original creative work had two important aspects: aesthetic symbols and their accompanying meanings. Over time decorative symbols and their meanings got divorced. Decorative symbols endured and were assisted by their aesthetic value to have eternal life. The art component was fossilized in so far as it continued to exist albeit without its original meanings. Because art was executed on utility objects which were changed but slowly, the draftspersons continued to produce the artifacts which they religiously aesthetically embellished, yet without any idea of the fundamental underlying meanings that resided in the art carried by the artifacts originally.

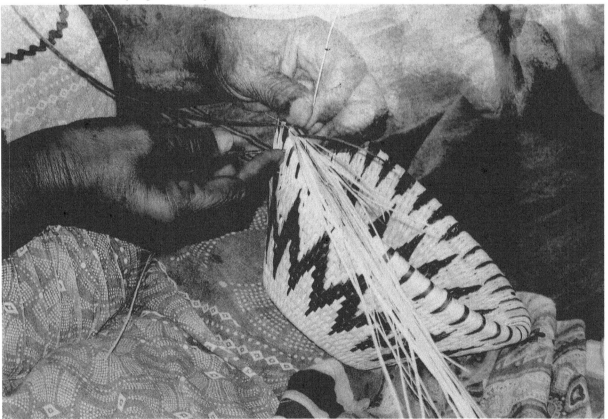

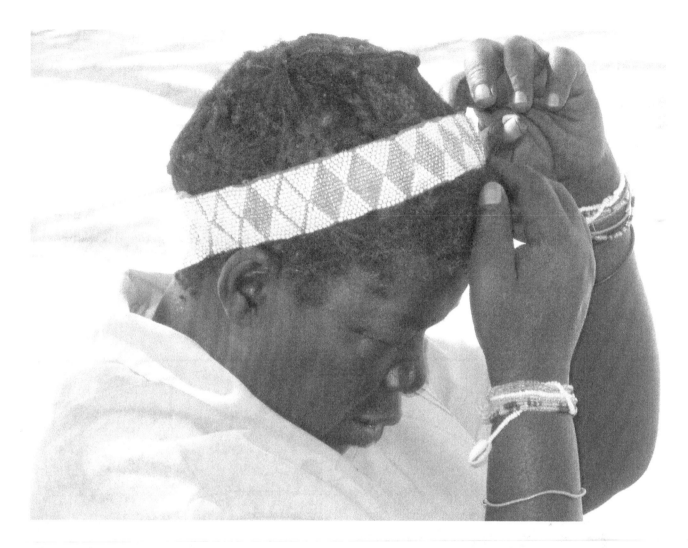

This is the situation today. The chevron decorative symbol, for example, is a compelling decorative symbol and graphic designers execute it on numerous materials without the slightest idea of the underlying meaning being conveyed by the decorative symbol which is pleasing visually. The chevron decorative symbol is executed on stone walls, on clay pots, on ilala baskets, on tie and dye materials and batik. The fossilized art requires to be distinguished from the artifacts that crafters make. Art requires a surface to carry it. In Africa the surfaces were provided by utility objects, artifacts that crafters made. African art resided in utility objects. A potter was at the same time an artist. While working on the pot, he/she is a craftsperson. The same person then becomes an artist. He did not pass the pot to another person who worked as an artist. There was no separation of functions or roles between artists and crafters. Fossilized art was however not left buried forever. It was excavated and reproduced on artifacts, albeit without the all-important attribute of creativity. This is what may be termed acts of reprography, or "duplicating" frozen art. True, the people engaging in this activity cannot be said to be artists. Art is never reproduced; works of art are different from each other at all times. This is an important aspect of creativity,

Crafters are purveyors of fossilized art and it is in this regard that they may not be referred to as artists. Further an artist is able to interpret his/her work. She knows the messages in her artwork. This is not the case with art reprography. Decorative symbols for example, are executed exquisitely without any knowledge of inherent messages and meanings they originally conveyed. A message not comprehended cannot be said to be conveyed; both the conveyor and the receiver must comprehend the message-encoding and decoding. The community of artists and consumers of their art should share something in common if they are to partake of the products of the former. Encoding and decoding of messages is resident within a community. When the processes are no longer taking place within a community, then it is difficult to say there is communication. Messages that are sent out must be received and interpreted. This is no longer the case with the decorative symbols. Emphasis now is on meaningless aesthetics, aesthetics that does not communicate; aesthetics for its intrinsic value which was never the case in traditional Africa.

Chevron symbols on the wall of the Great Enclosure at Great Zimbabwe.

What hope does Africa have to retrieve the lost messages that were originally infused into decorative symbols? It should never be surmised that because Africa did not write, so Africa had no means of documenting her experiences. It is only that her methodologies have been demonized and denigrated and are being replaced by Western epistemological traditions. One way that was used by Africa to pass down knowledge and information was what we may term spirit mediumship. When a person died their spirit got separated from the body which was interred. The spirit was, after a period of time, summoned to come back. The spirit then sought a living human medium through which it operated. The spirit spoke through the medium and possessed knowledge from the distant past. When the medium died, the spirit exited its abode and later took possession of another medium further down generations. Through the process, knowledge and information were passed down the generations. All this was in the realm of African Spirituality which is on the receiving end of proselytizing book religions, Christianity and Islam. As a result, an important spiritual epistemological mechanism of archiving and retrieving information and knowledge from the past is on a rapid decline. What this means in essence is that Africa cannot hope to access much of her cultural heritage which was archived through spiritual arrangement as its retrieval requires spiritual methodologies, which methodologies have been demonized, denigrated abd totally despised.

Control Tower at the Harare International Airport.

Western scholarship comes with attendant epistemological traditions. One of these is the need for researchers to undertake literature reviews and supervision by professors or doctors who have passed through the mill and ensure the novices are equally well grounded in western traditions of scholarship and academy. African epistemological traditions are trashed and demonized as unscientific. For example, spirit- mediumship which provided important intergenerational transmission channels for knowledge and information were trivialized and reduced to unscientific methodologies not worth investigation, let alone application by "civilized people." Sadly, African scholars fell for the trap and became willing participants in the destruction of African epistemological traditions. What we came to consider as scholarship was, in essence, an exercise in distancing oneself from African ways and methodologies. It was and is an adventure in negating African cosmologies, axiologies and aesthetics. The people who were expected to champion the African cause in terms of epistemology, axiology and cosmology became the most willing agents for the continent's demonization and delinking with her past traditions.

At the same time the messages resident in decorative symbols were lost in the mist of history. What may be celebrated as the successful conversion of the people of the "Dark Continent" is, in essence, the loss of Africa's cultural heritage, through delinking with its past. The channels for intergenerational transmission of knowledge and information and knowledge were severed. Western education and Christianity on the one hand and Islam on the other sought and succeeded in denigrating, demonizing and diminishing African beliefs and worldviews. Now with the African

Egyptian Pyramids

decorative designs facing a new thrust passing as "development", this is a new front where African cosmology is facing demise, even before its retrieval. The best that can be done now is to rediscover the original meanings resident in decorative symbols and have these preserved for posterity. The decorative symbols, on account of their compelling beauty and aesthetics, will continue to be executed on various materials. However, the challenge is to document the meanings and messages that were once conveyed by the decorative symbols. It is never too late to do so. African wisdom as witnessed through philosophy, astronomy, geometry and mathematics may, once again, be explored and revealed to the rest of the world.

Communication is inevitably accompanied by issues of moral ethics. In executing art, Africa was always cognizant of this. The visual arts were conditioned by and subjected to considerations of moral ethics. There was clarity with regard to what was right or wrong. Conveyed messages were in line with moral ethics. The content of messages was equally compliant. Moral ethics played an overarching, controlling and supervising role. The decorative symbols that we inherited should be subjected to the moral screening in order for them to be fully and accurately interpreted. The broader moral and ethical context should be considered lest we run the risk of misinterpreting Africa's decorative symbols.

We need to say why communication is important. What purpose did communication, regardless of the mode of communication, serve? One or more of these purposes were served by the decorative symbols. Africans were a people that sought group solidarity. The community was more important that the individual. A leading exponent of African Thought Professor John Mbiti expressed the idea succinctly. "I am because we are, and since we are, therefore I am." To maintain community spirit and build cohesion it is imperative that a common vision is inculcated and that is possible where there

Pyramid writing in Pharaoh's burial chamber.

is communication. Shared experiences help in building some esprit de corps which is important in working together to tackle challenging problems. Our past is made known to us when it is revealed to us. This can happen through interpretation of the decorative symbols. We get to know the cosmology of our ancestors, their aesthetics, beliefs and worldview. For example, in Egyptian pyramids there were symbols executed on walls within which the lifeless bodies of Pharaohs were deposited. The pyramid writing was meant to guide the departing spirit of a Pharaoh as it started out on a journey to some distant star. The ankh was one of the symbols which was executed which imparted eternal life to the spirit of a Pharaoh. Africans believed in communicating with the spiritual world through dreams. Through this medium the ancestors communicated various messages about the history of the people, the lost meanings of decorative symbols, herbs to use during healing of diseases, how to deal with epidemics, coming disasters and catastrophes such as impending wars. We have already made reference to spirit mediumship and how its waning role in African societies is witnessing the decline in the transmission of African heritage.

Related to dreams were omens. Certain events and happenings communicated the future; coming events such as the appearance of stars that told the wise men from the East about the birth of Jesus Christ. In the Christian world such revelations are acceptable. But lo and behold when Africa makes similar pronouncements these are regarded as superstitions without any substance. A man travelling on a journey got worried when a duiker, *impunzi* crossed his path ahead of him. He expected bad things to befall him during his journey. Some snakes such as the sand snake, *umhlwazi*, were interpreted as meaning the ancestral spirits were making known their arrival when such snakes entered a homestead. As a result such snakes were not chased away. The same was said to be true of a green *mamba*, *inyandezulu* entered a homestead. Snakes were associated with ancestral spirits and it comes as no surprise at all when San rock art depicts images of snakes. In fact, in the SiNdebele language the name for the ancestral spirits is the same as the word for snakes, *izinyoka*. There were events that were associated with or interpreted to mean something such as the death of a chief or king. For example, when Ndebele men went to war their wives rolled their sleeping mats and then leaned them against a wall in the hut where they slept. When the mat fell, it was interpreted to mean their husband had fallen in battle. Both cultural and natural phenomena were regarded as communicating something. All this was in order to protect the living by warning them of impending doom. To be forewarned is to be forearmed. Sometimes the messages being conveyed were pleasant ones. Each community had some data linking events to their meanings.

Proverbs and folktales were used to communicate important ideas that the community wished to inculcate in the minds of children. Moral codes were communicated through both proverbs and folktales. Certain community values such as honesty, truthfulness, kindness were emphasized through the use of characters in folktales who championed positive values. Similarly, negative values such as greed, cruelty, crookedness, inter alia, were exposed through characters who were punished for their wicked or antisocial deeds. Communication took various modes and served a purpose such as survival, socialization, entertainment and heritage transmission, inter alia.

However, decorative symbols were not the only mode of communicating ideas, values, ideals, principles and beliefs of communities that lived a long time ago. Orality or the spoken word was used by illiterate communities to communicate messages concerning various aspects of lived experiences.

Knowledge and information are the cementing blocks for a community or group of people. Both must be communicated to the younger generations so that their heritage is transmitted down the ages. Experiences gleaned from a people's heritage helps them to apply learned wisdom to solve current challenges. There is no need for them to reinvent the wheel. Heritage is important if a community is to survive and face the future with confidence.

We return to the chevron symbol once again. This is a decorative symbol that represents and was inspired by woman's body and the role she played in attaining continuity. A more detailed rendition will follow, but for now suffice it to say that Africa that we know would not have drawn female sex organs as that is not in line with African moral ethics. In any case, the important consideration was not in the sexual organs but in the all-important womb where fertilization, development of the zygote and embryo, nourishment, physical protection against shock and ultraviolet and infrared radiation took place. What is important to note here is that an interpretation of the chevron decorative symbol takes into account many factors, including cosmology, axiology, epistemology and aesthetics. The chevron decorative symbol will, of necessity, carry cosmological meanings infused into it by the community. At the same time, it would have been subjected to ethical and moral considerations. Equally, African aesthetical elements would be embraced, the most obvious one being repetition. It will be argued later that the chevron symbol is a unit which, if we wish to derive beauty out of, we get the unit repeated in a rhythmical and symmetrical way. All the elements that we have given here are an essential part of culture. In this regard, art is a cultural expression, one that brings to the fore a people's cosmology, axiology, epistemology and aesthetics. Both the content and technique of execution of the decorative symbols are important considerations and should be done on Africa's own terms. An Afro-centric view and perception is imperative.

Meaningful interpretation of Zimbabwe's decorative symbols should be a systematic effort that follows and takes on board certain principles which flow from African tenets. Many variables are at play. Careful scrutiny demands that many factors impinging on African attributes relating to cosmology, aesthetics and axiology, among others, are applied. As pointed out above, the chevron decorative symbol is not just about the cosmological thrust inherent within it. Equally, it is about applied ethics and morality and the attributes of African aesthetics. An interpretation subjected to the various principles stands a good chance of producing meaningful and sustainable interpretations. The least that should happen is the adoption of a pedestrian lackadaisical and halfhearted approach simply because we are dealing with issues African.

Chapter 2

DECORATIVE SYMBOLS:
SHARED VISUAL ART TRADITIONS AMONG ZIMBABWE'S ETHNIC GROUPS

Given Zimbabwe's ethnic diversity how possible is it to come up with decorative symbols for the whole country? Would this suggest decorative symbols for each of the ethnic groups? Apparently, this is not the position. When it comes to decorative symbols there are broad commonalities. In fact, this is true of the rest of the ethnic groups in black Africa, particularly those in southern Africa. In West Africa there are symbols for the Adinka tribe which are not found in central and southern Africa. This may possibly be a pointer to the peoples of African regions having separated a long time ago. As a result, they interacted with the environment, both human and physical, in different ways and that difference is captured in different symbols. However, this is not to say there are no commonalities. There are more commonalities than there are differences. At the level of the worldview and cosmology there are obvious commonalities. It is only that the key elements of worldview are represented by different symbols.

It is not skin colour that is shared in common by Africans. Rather, they share a common view of the world. They share a common cosmology, axiology and aesthetics. The manner in which these fundamental ideas are expressed may differ. Those are not the fundamentals but mere unique responses to different environments.

Most of the ethnic groups found in central and southern Africa belong to a group referred to as the Bantu. Their words for people/persons are very similar: e.g. abantu (Nguni), vanhu (Shona) and batho (Sotho/Tswana). Their designation as such indicates a shared history and culture at the highest level. It is possible too that they originate from the same source and came under the same environmental influences and hence their related languages and cultural practices, including the common decorative symbols. All the groups have a common architecture- cone on cylinder huts, circular byres and plan for the village layout. Virtually all of them make use of the chevron decorative symbol in the embellishment of their various artifacts.

Be that as it may, there are finer and yet minor differences that exist. These came about as a result of endogenous innovations in response to unique and peculiar environments. Similarly, their languages do have some minor differences that developed in response to local peculiarities that demanded local innovations but also to exogenous factors. Of interest to us are the ethnic groups in Zimbabwe who share a common culture of executing the same decorative symbols. Not only is the subject matter of decorative symbols shared in common, but so are the techniques of executing the said decorative symbols. Sometimes for reasons borne out of mischief, selfishness and divisiveness we have given unwarranted weight to superficial differences. Sometimes we fail to pin down the fundamentals but give emphasis to inconsequential differences.

For example, some people will see big differences between say, Great Zimbabwe and Old Bulawayo, King Lobengula's first capital town. And yet what leads them to arrive at such conclusions in type of materials used for building Great Zimbabwe, stones. Secondly, it is the size of the stone walls-massive by any measure! On the other hand at Old Bulawayo the perimeter walls were made from wood-not colossal for that matter. Our view is that what is more important and brings out the Africanness of the two settlements is how the different building materials are arranged. In both cases the designs are circular and this is typically African and yet the structures belong to Shona and Ndebele peoples who some people, for ill-informed and sometimes prejudicial reasons, see them as being very different. Where the Shona and Ndebele people used stones and wood respectively some groups used reeds or clay. In all instances the materials were subjected to African designs-circular in order to express fundamental African cosmology, worldview and beliefs.

The first black African people to inhabit Zimbabwe were the San, a hunter-gatherer group belonging to the Stone Age. Their tools were made of stone and their economies were built on hunting animals, by the men folk and gathering fruits, berries, tubers and roots by womenfolk. The San contributed to Zimbabwe's cultural heritage by bequeathing us with numerous galleries of exquisitely executed rock art. In terms of the visual art forms they too made use of the chevron symbol on ostrich egg shells and their leather attire. Their bows, as the name suggests, were curvilinear, one of the important attributes of African aesthetics. Their temporary shelters made from tree branches and grasses were hemispherical in shape, essentially meaning circular in design. Their art which they immortalized on sheltered rock surfaces showed scenes of individuals dancing in a circular formation. Very often history teachers will focus on differences between these Stone Age people and their Iron Age counterparts. Taking this route fails to appreciate the San as an African people who share a common cosmology aesthetics and morality and ethics, and axiology with the rest of the African groups who came after them. Therefore in terms of Africa's most basic designs, the circle and the chevron are shared in common by the Bantu and the San as African peoples that share common visual art forms and traditions that are informed by the same cosmological underpinnings. It is indeed correct to refer to Zimbabwe's decorative symbols that encompass the San. It is a pity though that they have been pushed to the periphery not only in physical or geographical terms but also in cultural terms. Sadly, the remnants of the San in the southwestern part of the country are so marginalized politically and culturally that they are not in a position, as a minority group, to bring to the fore their culture and worldview which are an integral part of Zimbabwe's cultural heritage, including the living traditions.

San hunters (L) Ostrich egg shell with chevron designs (R) (Delius 2007)

San shelter.

The group that arrived on Zimbabwean plane after the San hunter-gatherers were the Tonga who an at one time inhabited vast part of what has come to be known as Zimbabwe today. Sadly, some people have associated the Tonga with the remote, arid and hot Zambezi River valley. They ended up there as a result of being pushed there by the subsequent new arrivals: the Shona, Ndebele and whites. In actual fact the Tonga inhabited the central plateau of Zimbabwe. Kadoma is a Shona corrupted Tonga word for a flat-topped hill, katoma. Several names in Matabeleland North are of Tonga origin which is an indicator of some of the places that the Tonga ancestors inhabited: Dongamuzi (Dongamuse) Nkayi, Lupane, Panke and Mangangama, inter alia. The

Zezuru leather skirt with Chevron designs. (Dewey 1997)

Tonga shared a common cosmology with the rest of the Africans in Zimbabwe. Their huts display a circular deign, their hut doors bear the "twisted circle" or "endless/eternal knot" which is essentially a configured circle symbolizing eternity. The Venda door shares this symbol with the Tonga. The Ngoma Lungundu drum also bore the same symbol that expresses the idea of infinity. The beadwork of the Tonga women's skirts bore the chevron decorative symbol. The distinctive Tonga ilala baskets bore the chevron decorative symbol while the basket itself has a circular design which is true of their clay pots too.

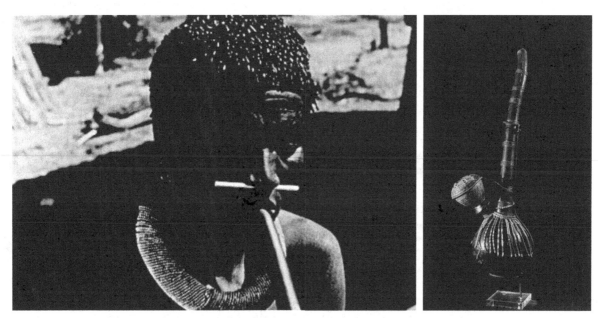

Tonga woman (L) Tonga smoking pipe (R) (Dewey 1997)

The mighty Zambezi River also carries a lot of symbolism among the BaTonga. The river is viewed as a source of livelihoods. The big river, mulonga mupati, has made it possible for the BaTonga to cultivate crops twice a year. In addition to this more literal perception the Zambezi River is symbolic of a phallic object (male sex organ) which engages Mother Earth (female) in an eternal erotic embrace (see Preface). The symbolized sexual act represents eternity. *"Ukuzala yikuzelula,"*implies as indicated above the idea of continuity which is the recurring African theme behind the decorative symbols in their various configurations and manifestations. The water-bearing river fertilizes the earth, which then gives forth food, for example fish and crops growing on the alluvial soils, on which the Tonga subsist.

Binga is a good example of where the design of the Tonga baskets has been tempered with in the name of "development". International markets with a different worldview have led to the BaTonga women working with foreign artists in an effort to meet aesthetic demands of a different group of people overseas. The BaTonga, most of whom did not comprehend the messages on their crafts, are now having to execute new designs about whose messages and meanings they are equally blank. Furthe, the new designs and decorative symbols are not in line with the attributes of African aesthetics. Methodologies of crafting and materials used are what will ultimately remain of the visual art traditions of the BaTonga. What can be said though is that the BaTonga are being delinked and uprooted from their past, a past captured, enshrined and expressed in their visual art traditions and other forms of artistic expressions. He who pays the piper certainly calls the tune. The best that can be done now is to explore and document the messages resident in their decorative symbols so that as they migrate from the circular baskets and their accompanying decorative designs they will appreciate where they are coming from.

The BaTonga arrived on the Zimbabwean scene before 800 AD and the next group, the Shona arrived about

Khami monument

1000 AD. Like the BaTonga, they too were an Iron Age people who distinguished themselves as builders of settlements with stone walls. They had acquired the knowledge to sculpt stones: over the years they became polished stone masons. The stone walls, masvingo, were first built at

Mapungubgwe near the confluence of the Limpopo and Shashe (*kushaya Ishe*) rivers. Stone masonry was at the time not that refined. Crudely hewn stones were piled up, with at least two stone walls around each hill settlement. The walls enclosed typical Kalanga cone-on-cylinder huts made from clay, wood and grass thatch. In the Kalanga language a settlement, village, of this nature was called 'nzi'. These 'nzi' were of stone, in reference to the walls and NOT huts or houses of stone. However, more recent research by Chirikure, a Zimbabwean archaeologist seems to point to Mapela as the proto 'nzi wa mabgwe', the village of stones. A marked departure from previous tradition is, in the African sense, captured in naming. The practice is in vogue to this day. The Ndebele will refer to the first homestead roofed with iron sheets as '*umuzi wamazenge*', the homestead with iron sheets. Note that the naming of a village in such a case may be informed by the construction of huts, the nature or magnitude of perimeter walls or any other part of 'nzi' which is unique and a departure from previous tradition. Certainly, the stone settlements were a new tradition which was a marked departure from previous architectural traditions. One would thus have expected the change to be captured in the naming of the village, 'nzi'. In this particular case there was marked departure in terms of walls of stone, it was inevitable that the 'nzi' would be qualified as '*nzi wa mabgwe.*' Our argument is that this is the word, albeit slightly modified, that gave the name to the nation of

Conical tower at Great Zimbabwe.

Zimbabwe. The confusion came about as a result of ignoring the Tjikalanga language which is the language most representative of the language spoken then.

Apparently, it was a whole region incorporating areas to the north of both Mapela, Sebirwa word for dassie, which had rudimentary stone walls. The areas include the following hills: Lubhangwe, Takaliyawa, Halisupi, Sankonjana (where Pathisa was born and grew up), Mazambane, and Gobadema, extending up to Shape River a tributary of the Mwewu River, itself a tributary of the Tuli River.

Stone wall on Mapungubwe hill

The question that begs an answer is why did building in stone start then and there? This may be a difficult question to answer though we do know that it was trade with the East Coast that led to the accumulation of wealth in the regions where stone walling started. Gold was being traded initially by the Arab Moors and later the Portuguese. Gold found at Mapungubgwe carried the signature of gold from the Gwanda gold belt to the north. Gold and ivory were the key products being traded in the interior in exchange for calico and glass beads. The Limpopo River

Checkered board on a stone wall at Khami monument

valley provided the trade route from the Indian Ocean settlements into the interior and smaller rivers provided access to the various smaller settlements dotted in the areas mentioned above. Some of the rivers are: Tuli, Shashane, Kafusi, Tudi, Mkhobothi and Pelele plus a few others, all ultimately pouring their rivers into the Shashe River. The area of interest seems to have been defined by the presence of gold at Legion Mine (Gatsane) New Mine (east of Tshelanyemba), to the west and Mandihongola-Gobadema belt) to the north and Gwanda itself further to the north.

However, for our purposes the Bakalanga-Shona groups produced a wide range of artifacts that bore the same decorative symbols in common with other ethnic groups. Even their latest additions to their material culture, the stone walls, became surfaces where decorative symbols were executed.

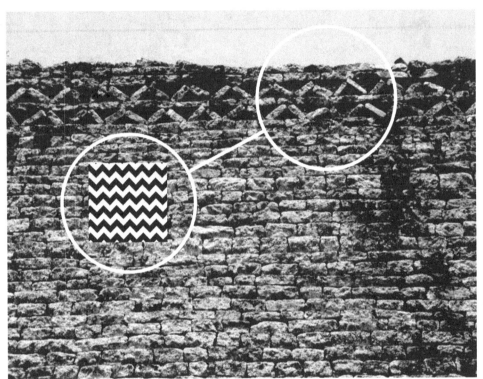

Chevron symbols on the wall at Great Zimbabwe.

While the earlier walls such as those in the areas mentioned above did not bear any decorative symbols subsequent walls were exquisitely decorated, a phenomenon which seemed to tally with the period when the walls were constructed. The most recent walls were the best decorated: Khami (Nkame we wepfumba dzisina mhulu), Naletale. Dlodlo (Danga le ngombe/Danangombe) and Zinjanja (Regina). The intermediate walls such as those at Great Zimbabwe were moderately decorated. The quality of stone masonry also matched the period of construction of the walls. The art of carving stone improved as time went by. Both Khami and Naletale bore a large variety of decorative symbols: chevrons, checked/chess board, herring bone, cord and dentelle.

Kalanga-Shona items of material culture that bore decorative symbols included the following among several others: clay pots, interior hut walls, leather aprons for women, battle axes(makano/humbwa), beadwork, headdress(ngundu), ceremonial walking sticks, stools, wooden headrests, snuff boxes, hand pianos(mbira), scabbard (bakatwa), spear handles, wooden drums, inter alia.

Chevron designs at the National Heroes Acre in Zimbabwe

The National Heroes Acre in Zimbabwe was inspired by the Great Zimbabwe monument and bears the decorative symbols from several ethnic groups in Zimbabwe. As to how much we are able to interpret the meanings of the chosen decorative symbols is a contested issue. In some instances weirdest attempts at interpretation have been proffered, attempts that did not seem to take on board the cosmology, axiology, epistemology and aesthetics of the Bantu people of Zimbabwe who are the originators of the decorative symbols. Further, creating the decorative symbols was a balancing act between aesthetic execution in line with attributes of African beauty, infusion of cosmological meanings and operating within the limits set by moral ethics. For some unknown reason there does not seem to be some sense of urgency to try and interpret the decorative symbols. Design in general seems to be influenced by the very same considerations behind the decorative symbols. It only makes sense to seek out their meanings and document these for posterity. Our cultural heritage and its deeper meanings will be appreciated better. At the political level it is this pan-Zimbabwean, indeed pan-African commonality that should inspire unity among the seemingly diverse ethnic groups. At the most critical levels we find unity among the various Zimbabwean ethnic groups. We can only build on this common sense of belonging together which is manifested in the visual art traditions of our decorative symbols.

When Mfecane took place in South Africa the Babirwa, a Sotho group originally belonging to the generic Bakalanga group pushed further north from the Limpopo Province of South Africa to south-western Zimbabwe. They arrived at the time when the Lozwi/Rozvi were the rulers. They settled, in the first quarter of the 19th Century, in areas south of Gwanda (Nyathi, 2015) . A lot of names in the areas where they settled bear names from their language which is an amalgam of Pedi, Tswana and Tjikalanga. They too produced items of material culture.

Chevron symbols on diagnostic ivory tablets.

The Ndebele were the last African group to arrive on the Zimbabwean scene in about 1840. The Nguni group under the leadership of King Mzilikazi Khumalo had strong traditions of executing decorative symbols. As was the case with earlier groups, the circular design was applied in the making of artifacts and hut architecture, designs of cattle byres, and village layouts. The chevron was executed on their headrests *(imithiya)*, mats *(amacansi)* and in particular their ilala baskets *(ingcebethu)*. Though these people were coming into Zimbabwe from the south where they were part of the Nguni group their visual art traditions were no different from those of their earlier counterparts in terms of subject/thematic content and techniques of execution.

It is these similarities that make it possible to refer to Zimbabwe's decorative symbols that have the same subject content, that is, the meanings and messages borne by the decorative symbols. In their southward migration from the north the Nguni left some remnants in Zimbabwe who were subsequently incorporated by the incoming Bakalanga/Shona groups. Aeneas Chigwedere (1980) identifies these people as the Dziva/Siziba Hungwe/Nyoni group. This may not make sense to some people simply because the Nguni in general discarded their totems ad came to use the first names of their ancestors. For example, Khumalo is the first name of an ancestor, so is Gumede, Mkhwananzi, Zulu, Mabhena and many others. There are some who though they made use of the first names of their ancestors they still remembered their totems. Mkhwananzi will remember he is Nkwali abd therefore Nyoni, and so does Mthethwa, who is Nyambose. What is a big lie is the claim that the Nguni did not have totems. ALL the Bantu had totems. What happened to the Nguni is happening to other people even today. The Nyathis in Zimbabwe have one section of them who have come to be known as Mabusa and another called Mpabanga. In years to come it may not be known that they are Nyathi.

Chapter 3

DECORATIVE SYMBOLS:
SURFACES ON WHICH THEY WERE MADE AND THE TECHNIQUES OF EXECUTION

Decorative symbols are executed on various surfaces. The said surfaces are those of utility objects. The primary aim was the crafting of an artifact that had some functional use. The surfaces, like a teacher's chalk board, were used to carry a secondary function, the posting of decorative symbols, though too carrying out a function-that of transmitting messages through an aesthetic medium. Whatever object it was, it had its beauty enhanced and its overall presentability captured the eyes of he/she who used the object. A wooden plate, with or without embellishment, serves food. However, when a wooden plate carries decorative symbols it feeds the body in a physical sense but also attends to the aesthetic needs of the mind. Some objects are made to serve in the spiritual realm. When they are decorated they please the ancestral spirits even more.

At the same time we should appreciate that the objects carry a bit of aesthetics even before they are decorated. This is because the artifacts exhibit some attributes of African aesthetics. The design of the objects is circular, and circularity is an important African aesthetic attribute. There is also an element of functionality. Moving objects require a circular design. Cosmic bodies, which have a circular design, are in constant and regular/rhythmic motion around elliptical orbits. It has been observed that traditional Africans sought to replicate the cosmos on their own prealm of existence. Not only did they emulate the circularity that characterizes the cosmos but they also sought to express its continuity. To the African the cosmos have no known beginning and it is assumed they have no imaginable end. Even as we write the biggest object in the cosmos, much bigger than the Milky Way, has been discovered and named BOSS. The cosmos thus embrace the idea of eternity, infinity, perpetuity, continuity which attributes are pinned down to constant change within the context of movement. Birth, life, death and rebirth are inherent within this constant change as indicated through the movement of the moon. The sun too rises, reaches its zenith and begins the process of setting and ultimately night falls which wanes till the sun raises, (rebirth) and grows and develops and its advance is seen as complete when day is at its maximum.

This cycle of birth-growth-development-decay-death and rebirth was closely observed by Africans. Death is not the end but a necessary component if eternity is to be achieved. Death was thus welcomed as a prelude to life in another realm. Traditional Africans even tied their cultural practices to the cosmic realities that they observed. The timing of cultural practices was in relation to the stages in the never ending cycles found within the cosmos. The traditional doctors had their operations linked to the lunar cycle. Their spiritual powers increased and decreased in tandem with the changing lunar cycles or phases. As a result, cultural activities were designed into phases that were in consonant with the phases of some chosen cosmic bodies. For example, individuals undergoing spiritual initiation graduated when the constellation Pleicedes, *isilimela* appeared. Some agricultural practices such as planting were timed to coincide with the full moon. Inxwala among the Nguni peoples was held at full moon. The Ngoni of Chief Mphezeni in Chipata, Zambia always hold their Inchwala(Inxwala) towards the end of February each year When the cosmos are at their best in terms of energies, cultural practices made to coincide with these also acquired the energy and vibrancy of the cosmos with which they had been timed or married.

In African terms the circular design is beautiful. The setting sun bears testimony to that. The rising sin is equally beautiful by virtue of its colour and also its shape. When the moon rises in the western sky its crescent shape is pleasant to the discerning eye. A full circle or part of it, the crescent or curvilinear shape, is artistic. To the African this contrasts sharply with the rectangular designs whose shape does not appeal and is not represented at the cosmic level. As a result, Africans did not make artifacts that were rectangular or bore right angles. Their huts, cattle byres and other structures bear testimony to this. Their artifacts were smoothened off to give them a rounded off (circular) appearance.

African ideas of a beautiful lady embraced one with a full figure, meaning she has enhanced circular features in terms of breasts, waist and bums. African eyes were trained to appreciate the beauty inherent in objects displaying a circular design. A functional object performed a desired function while simultaneously exhibiting characteristics of beauty. This means, from the outset functionality and aesthetics were married. Embellishing a utility object added to its beauty in a bigger way. However, it is important to appreciate that beauty was not for emotional consumption. Beauty performed a certain role-it communicated certain messages to its consumers. In that regard, it was functional, the debate may lie in which between beauty and functionality was the more primary. In essence therefore, there are two levels within a decorated artifact displaying marriages between functionality and aesthetics. One arrives at the conclusion that each, functionality and aesthetics, never had a separate and distinct existence. The two always occurred together, or coexisted. When it is said Africa never had art for art's sake this is true when we realize that art and functionality always occurred together.

It is this African reality that is changing. More and more objects are being produced for their aesthetic value. Functionality has been taken off and substituted by objects made either from plastic or metal. When African designs are being replaced by Western ones, the loss that the African artifact endures is at both aesthetic and functional levels. The artifacts already were decorative or aesthetic. The baskets being produced no longer fulfilled any known functional roles. After that only aesthetics at design level remained. That too is now going and what may remain for a while is aesthetics emanating from decorative symbols on functionless artifacts. For how long the decorative symbols will hold out remains to be seen. Soon the crafters may be cajoled to execute decorative symbols that are in line with dictates from the world of those controlling the financial markets. Purse strings will destroy both African functionality and aesthetics.

Baskets with rectangular designs (Lupane Women Centre)

Before proceeding we need to indicate other traits of African aesthetics in addition to circularity. Repetition is an important attribute in African aesthetics. The circle does carry that trait but may not be as obvious as in a chevron symbol. The latter is an upward looking V or a triangle. As a single design the chevron is not beautiful. To lend beauty to it the unit is repeated. Even in dance performances the idea of repetition is evident. Dancing consists of repeated movements which may go on and on till, in the case of spiritual dancers, the individual gets possessed. The chevron displays repetition at the cultural level, a phenomenon copied from natural cosmic reality. Repetition adds beauty but will also link man to the cosmos. Spiritual dancing connects an individual to one of the cosmic orbits. This is captured in the rock art of the San.

The curvilinear shape, represented by the crescent moon, is another attribute of African aesthetics. A line that bends in a circular manner is beautiful to gaze. Modern designers are using the design more and more for its beauty. Many traditional artifacts displayed the curvilinear design and that imparted beauty to the objects.

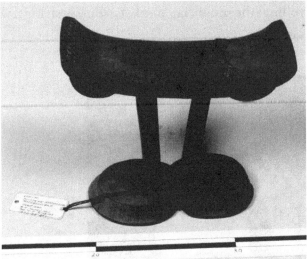

Bench design appropriated from a headrest (Amanzi Restaurant, Harare)

Movement is easier to glean in the chevron symbol. The movement is not haphazard. Rather, it is rhythmic. Regular movement or change is an important attribute in African aesthetics. The circle itself carries that characteristic, though it may not be that easily discernible. Nature is characterized by rhythm. The seasons are rhythmic. Day and night, the diurnal cycle is equally rhythmic. The lunar cycle is rhythmic. Rhythm is associated with movement, regular and predictable movement. African music and dance are rhythmic and that lends beauty to the music and the dance.

Dancers during the Jikinya Traditional Dance Festival.

In the visual arts, symmetry, the equitable distribution of arts elements is an important attribute in African aesthetics. The chevron displays the trait very well. Related to symmetry is equilibrium. Both qualities exhibit beauty and aesthetics. In all these attributes movement is underlined. The attributes are in reality attributes of movement. They describe movement, the type of movement and its traits.

The decorative symbols that exhibited beauty were executed on surfaces of artifacts: wood, leather, stone, ivory, egg shell, clay, grass and gourd. The question now is how the decorative symbols were executed on these surfaces provided by the crafts.

Decorative symbols were executed in such a way that they lasted a very long time. The messages that they carried were encoded from time immemorial. For a while the decorative symbol and its meaning co-existed. Over the years the meanings were lost, leaving the symbols to endure on the basis of their aesthetic appeal. We can now rely on the echoes from a distant past, however faint they may be, to piece together decorative symbols and their original messages. Materials on which symbols were made differed in terms of perishability. Unfired clay perishes more readily than fired clay. Archaeologists have retrieved fired shards with eternal symbols. How long a symbol lasts depends on the nature of material that makes the object, Wood is readily perishable, so is leather, grass and to some extent, horn. Stone, ivory and fired clay are more durable and have been used by historians and archaeologists to get glimpses into the cultures of communities that lived where the artifacts were retrieved.

A good example is the "My Beautiful Home-*Comba Indlu Ngobuciko*" where women in the northern part of Matobo District decorate their houses using natural pigments excavated from the ground. The walls become exquisite but only for a short period. House decorations are done in the winter months when there are no rains. As soon as the rains come the water soluble pigments are washed away. The women have to start all over again the following year. All the beautifully executed designs are lost. When baskets age and get discarded they go with their decorative symbols. The symbols that stand a chance to last are those executed on rock or stone. A good example is the soapstone birds found at Great Zimbabwe. Soapstone diagnostic dishes, also found at Great Zimbabwe, have stood the test of time. Divination/diagnostic ivory tablets have preserved some designs which are not necessarily decorative but all the same communicate messages that traditional doctors are able to decipher or decode.

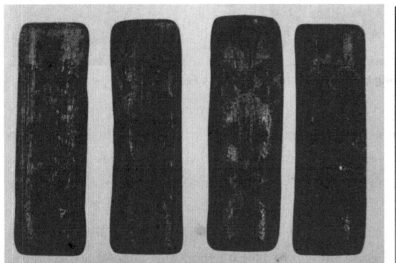 

Chevron symbols on ivory diagnostic tablets (L) (Ellert 2002) and the Zimbabwe bird (R)

Some designs are not executed on surfaces of objects or structures. Instead, they become part of the object. The walls at Great Zimbabwe have decorative symbols crafted in such a way they become an integral part of the wall. The symbols stand out on account of differing stones used, such as colour where dark dolerites produce dark bands. When stones are arranged in a particular structural way they produce patterns that stand out, e.g. herringbone, cord, dentelle and checked (chess) board and dentelle. Such arrangements that constitute decorative symbols at Great Zimbabwe have endured almost two centuries of weathering.

Painted symbols on protected rock surfaces also have produced enduring images from which we can glean African heritage. The San hunter-gatherers have excelled in this regard. Protected caves eliminate rain and marked diurnal temperature fluctuations. This explains the lasting durability of rock art though now people who do not appreciate the value resident in rock art are defacing the priceless images that tell stories from the African past.

Rock art depicting San hunters.

How were the images or decorative symbols executed on various objects? The first surface that humanity had access to was his/her own skin. He/she made inscriptions on the skin and introduced black or other pigments to stand out against the background of the skin. Engraving or the making of incisions, *inhlanga/nyora*, especially if infused with coloured pigments lasted long. Incisions so made served as tribal marks that differentiated one group from the other. In some cases they were made when individuals reached a certain stage in their development such as when they reached puberty or when they got married. These were the equivalent of milestones in one's development journey. Women among the BaTonga used to make incision on their bellies. Among the VaNjanja of Buhera iron smelters made iron furnaces with scarifications as a way of indicating that the furnaces symbolized femininity, women with prominent pyramidal breasts. Sometimes incisions conveyed the idea of beauty. Zulu women made cuttings in their skins and introduced cow dung into them. These lasting swellings called *amancumpa* imparted beauty to the ladies. Clay pots were also provided with these swellings made by introducing small lumps of clay. The swellings were also called *amansumpa* and enhanced the beauty of the Zulu clay pots, especially of the Magwaza community in KwaZulu-Natal. While engravings and incisions ended with shallow depressions, *amansumpa* on the other hand were raised lumps. In both cases sharp objects such as thorns, sharpened sticks or sharpened pointed metals were used. Apparently, Africans were labeled as a primitive people when they did this. Now tattooing has been taken on board by other races and they do not apply the label "primitive" to themselves. Engraving has been executed on rock surfaces in South Africa. Engraved chevrons have been found in Mpumalanga Province of South Africa. Gourds were also engraved in the same fashion as clay pots when still wet. The latter required sharp metallic objects to cut into the gourd and execute desired symbols.

Rock and pot engravings (Delius, 2007).

Painting was another technique used to execute decorative motifs. Pigments mixed with water were used. For example, Ndebele women painted their faces during ceremonies such as weddings or when amalobolo were being paid. Butholezwe Kgosi Nyathi wrote as follows on Amagugu International Heritage Centre Face Book Page:

In an endeavour to add ambience to the My Beautiful Home awards ceremony a face painting contest was conducted. This was the second edition of the face painting competition the first such contest was held in 2014 also during the occasion of the My Beautiful Home awards ceremony. But of course emphasis is not on the competition itself, but the desire to revitalize and preserve cultural heritage

Face painting, like hut decoration, is done using natural pigments. Different colours of soil - black, yellow and red - are crushed and sifted into fine powder. Ash is also often used. One of the soil colors is applied in powder form on the face as an undercoat. The other types of soil are then mixed with water and various patterns are then imprinted on the face.

Face painting is not an individual effort as one's face is designed by another woman. While the painter in some instances conceptualizes the design, in other instances the one being painted describes the art they want on their face. The artist, ultimately, is the one who does the actual painting. Some women extend the painting beyond the face to the upper torso of their bodies In the Ndebele past; face painting was largely done during social gatherings such as weddings.

Face painting during My Beautiful Home Project.

Natural pigments were water soluble and therefore did not last if executed on surfaces not protected from rain. The San however made use of pigments mixed with substances that lasted long such as egg white, sap from some trees and blood. Clay pots were burnished using black lead, a practice that still persists in Masvingo near Great Zimbabwe. Burnishing could be perceived as a form of painting.

As pointed out above some decorative symbols were built into the walls such as at Great Zimbabwe. Both the construction method and the fact that the wall was made from rock ensured that the decorative symbols lasted as long as the walls stood. The same was true when plaiting baskets. The way ilala fibre was coiled around the core of grass produced patterns that stood out against the rest of the surface of the basket. One such arrangement in the coiling of Ndebele and

Tswana baskets was called *umsisi*. Also related to these forms of execution was moulding in particular in so far as the clay pots were concerned. By adding clumps of clay desired patterns were executed which when dry became a permanent component of the clay pot. The arrangement was even more permanent when the structure was fired.

Where knitting was done, change in direction of warps created an outstanding pattern. A different texture, colour or relief has been used to execute decorative symbols on some artifacts. Colour arrangements in beadwork have produced decorative symbols.

Minister Abigail Damasane during My Beautiful Home prize giving ceremony

Sandra Ndebele-Sibindi.

Finally, let us mention tying and dying and batik as techniques that were, and still are, used to execute decorative symbols.

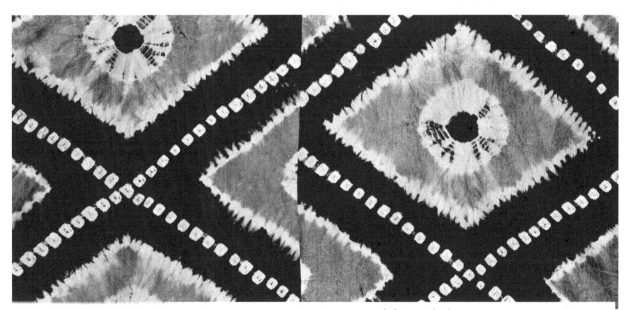

Chevron designs produced using tye and dye technique.

Chevron designs on batik material.

Wiring, by using brass or copper wire was applied on artifacts such as the scabbard (bakatwa) snuff boxes (nhekwe) and battle axes (imbemba/makano/humbwa).

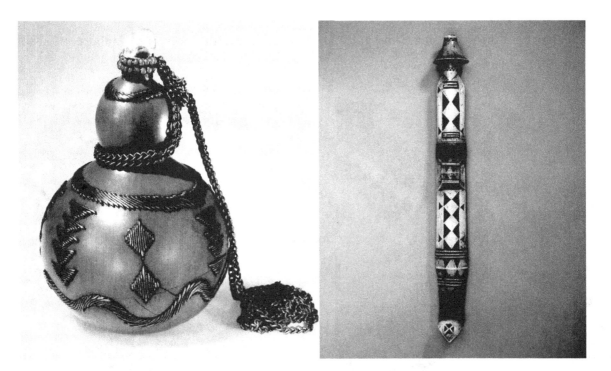

Gourd snuff box with Chevron wire decorations (L) Scabbard with Chevron Designs. (R) (Dewey, 1997)

Now we turn to the decorative symbols and attempt interpreting the messages that they bear. Background information supplied above should facilitate easier grasp of interpretations being proffered.

Chapter 4

GEOMETRIC DECORATIVE SYMBOLS

1 The circle

"Summer kills autumn and is itself killed by winter," says a Seneca legend. The circle seems to be the basic organizing form in the universe. Cosmic bodies are circular in design and all of them are in constant motion along elliptical orbits. Closer home, within our own Milky Way galaxy the sun is circular and has a number of planets that are orbiting it. Once again, the orbits are essentially circular. Where there is movement a circular design is inevitable. When the wheel was discovered in the cultural sector it already existed in nature. A rectangular shape does not seem to facilitate movement. The principles of aerodynamics seem to demand that objects in motion be circular in shape. Both cars and airplanes have acquired that design to facilitate motion.

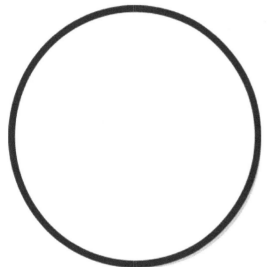

A close look at nature will reveal that many objects are circular in design. If we understand that something cylindrical comprises an infinite number of circles or rings then it will be easier to appreciate the proliferation of the circle and its myriad of varied representations. The leaves on trees are circular. Wind, ice and water produce circular physical landscapes e.g. sand dunes, cirque, U-valleys, meandering rivers and ox-bow lakes, inter alia. Human beings themselves are created on the circular design-are we not cylindrical? Are our intestines not tubular? Is a tube not the same as a hollow cylinder? What about body apertures, are they not circular-do not be confused by their shape when in a resting position. We could go on and on and what will become apparent is that human beings are circular in shape. It is not just the Planet Earth that is circular but the flora and fauna on it are equally circular in design. You only need to be more perceptive.

Would it come as a wonder to see the African adopt the circular design as his basic ordering unit at the level of cultural domain? Some mischievous and ignorant person thought he was insulting the African when he said the African had a "circular mentality." Obviously the person belonged to the group that perceives development in a linear sense. He was not aware that the entire universe is, mutatis mutandis, circular in design. What God created was circular in design. The more godly Africans followed suit and built their huts following the same design; their cattle byres were also circular. Their artifacts were also designed to emulate the natural design and be in line with it. It was this desire to copy nature that saw the African seek to preserve the environment on which he recognized his dependence. Looking around nature, the African failed to see the right angle. How could he produce on the cultural front what he did not see in nature? A long time ago early man made use of the circular design. In Rome the ruined Coliseum is circular in design. The Stonehenge in England was no different. "The most noticeable structure that we see at Stonehenge today is a circle of upright sarsens with some surviving horizontal lintels perched on top of them(Pearson 2012: 27)." African village layout was circular in design with the Ndebele and Zulu settlements comprising concentric circles of palisades. The circular design pervaded within the village. In addition to layout, huts were circular-both the walls and roofs(as long as you appreciate that a cone is in actual fact a series of circles of declining or increasing radii or diametre). Inside the hut was a hearth, also circular in design. The three chosen hearthstones were also circular. The various artifacts within the hut were circular in design-notably the clay pots, ilala baskets, straining baskets, winnowing baskets and many others. The African observed too that some natural objects that he used with minimal cultural intervention were circular in design: the ladle he fashioned from gourd and the calabash for storing water or curdled milk, *amasi*. Everywhere the theme was the circular design.

What did the African see from nature that he sought to replicate on the cultural front? The cosmos was characterized by movement, that is, constant change which in the final analysis led to eternity or infinity of the cosmos. This was something positive that the African did well to copy. He wanted eternal life. Among the Ndebele the origin myth tells the story of a chameleon that was sent to tell people they were going to have eternal life. As things turned out the chameleon failed to take the good message on time till the Creator sent lizard, *untulo*, with the message that people should die. Eternity, which is an attribute of the cosmos, is what the African sought. Even when it comes to his business ventures he wants these to flourish eternally. Ritual murders are motivated by this desire. Within a human being the only cells with generative power are reproductive cells, sperms and ova. Sadly, a whole big man must be killed in order to get the sex organs within which reside the required cells. Continuity at the level of a people is unthinkable in the absence of sexual reproduction.

While in humans sexual reproduction lay at the heart of attaining continuity, at the environmental or cosmic level that quality was achieved through cyclical movement that displays birth-growth-development-decay-death-rebirth. The cycle goes on and on, ad infinitum. Both the sun and the moon are in constant motion during which the above cycle is evident. Continuity or endlessness is the resulting state. The circle therefore is that design that symbolizes continuity, eternity, infinity, fertility, immortality, endlessness and imperishability. The African looked at both human sexuality and its equivalent in the cosmos. In the former, woman played a bigger role than man. Beyond the sexual act the rest of the process was left to the woman to shoulder. The man's job in the procreative process was done and finished. Even insects knew that and hence after mating some female insects turned around and devoured male partners. Their work had been accomplished and could, at this juncture, become a good source of protein for eggs growing within the body of the female insect.

The observed phenomena that led to eternity incorporated the cycle. It comes as no surprise that the circular design was adopted to impart the same trait on the cultural front. Further, eternity at human level was achieved more by women than men. It was only expected that the African was going to assign the circle as a design for eternity and have it symbolize woman as will become apparent when we deal with the chevron symbol. The circle therefore represents woman who represents continuity and endlessness.

We need to make a further observation in relation to how women were perceived by traditional Africans. There was also a link between them and the cosmos as common players in the game of bringing about the much desired continuity. As pointed out above, the cosmos attained continuity through movement which resulted in regeneration and rebirth. There was cyclical movement. The women too were seen as having that cosmic quality which was unique to them and not men. There was that obvious link with the moon. We did point our earlier that the terms for menstrual flow in several languages in Zimbabwe and the southern region in general were the same as the name for the moon (*inyanga/mwedzi*): *usenyangeni* ("she is on the moon"), "*arikumwedzi*" ("she is on the moon"). The moon, *inyanga/mwedzi*, through its lunar cycle, embraced rebirth (appearance of the new moon)-growth and development-degeneration- decay-death-rebirth. This is the cycle of life which incorporates death. This is the phenomenon that leads to infinity, eternity and immortality. Only woman possesses this quality through her menstrual cycle that linked her to the moon in terms of regeneration (rebirth) and degeneration (death). Interestingly, the two cycles last 28 days. Man, on the other hand, lacks this type of link to the cosmic quality of regeneration/rebirth. It was only proper that African selected decorative symbols inspired by woman, the earthly counterpart to the cosmos to symbolize continuity and infinity. It was a recognition that lent respect to the womenfolk. As we shall see, there were hardly any decorative symbols depicting the idea of continuity that depicted males. Only to a much lesser extent were men participants in the attainment of continuity. If insects knew it would our ancestors have failed to see it?

How are we to perceive the circle? The circle represents movement or constant change. The movement is rhythmic or regular. A circle has no beginning or end. That way, it symbolizes eternity and continuity. One could say the circle symbolizes "sexual reproduction" within the cosmos. At the human level the cosmos is replicated through the same phenomenon in which the woman plays a bigger role. In fact, as it turns out, Africa recognized the bigger role played by her women folk. They were at the centre of the attainment of continuity and eternity. What happened, when it h. We here refer to the marginalization of African women. As we shall see below, most if not all, geometric decorative symbols emphasized the all-important role of women as the key players in attaining continuity and eternity. In nature there are trees that do not bear fruits and others that do. Trees that bear fruit are said to be female and those that do not are male, at least this is the position among the Ndebele. This gives greater emphasis to women as being at the centre of the natural process that brings about continuity. The circle is thus the symbol for Mother Earth who is

female, the woman who is the dimunitive of Mother Earth and the idea of continuity. The greater Mother Earth is the source of all sustenance. Like a mother, the earth can feed everyone through the crops it produces. Cycles are the mothers of eternity and continuity. Smaller "Mothers Earth" are fed by this Mother Earth and then feed their babies, initially through the placenta while they are still in the womb and through suckling from the breasts once born. The chain of women sustaining life on earth was recognized by traditional Africans who created the decorative symbols. Mother Earth, Human Mother and continuity constitute an important life-giving trilogy.

We should observe that the circle was used both as an ordering design and a decorative symbol. Objects that bear decorative symbols are circular in design. Hut walls were circular and bore other forms of decorative symbols. The artifacts, while some of them carried circular decorative symbols, were the ones that were resplendent with the decorative symbols such as the chevrons. Variety is the spice of life. This was true of decorative symbols. One form was presented in a variety of configurations and still carried the same meaning or message. The circle was never presented in the same form. Instead, it was configured to achieve variety and eliminate monotony. The meaning remained the same as we shall see below.

The circle is sometimes perceived as ouroboros a snake that tries to bite its own tail-a circular serpent. The resulting circular design represents the cycle of life, the idea of eternity or continuity. The idea here is that the sun rises every day. There will be another day tomorrow (Etu ece o'du ku Lugbaa, Uganda)

In conclusion, let us bring out the symbolism exhibited by the circle in terms of how the community and society were organized. Group or community solidarity was emphasized. Human interaction was equally emphasized. People exhibited some esprit de corps. The circle captured these important community values.

2 Variations of the circle

a) Curvilinear

Sometimes a circle is not rendered in full. A part of it suffices and represents the moon when it appears on the western sky. As pointed out above, the curvilinear shape is one of the attributes of African aesthetics. Its significance lies in its similarity to the new moon which symbolizes rebirth/regeneration which comes after death. The cycle of life (continuity/eternity) is subsumed in that design and that cycle. Essentially, therefore, the curvilinear shape is a part of the circle and symbolizes exactly that which the circle symbolizes. At the level of artifacts the curvilinear decorative design is found on the headrests of both the Ndebele and the Shona. The assumption here is that what starts off as a curvilinear shape will progress till it is a full circle. This we learn from the new moon. It starts off as a curvilinear shape (crescent moon), then grows as it waxes till it is a full moon. A crescent moon is a common feature on the flags of Arab nations. Usually the crescent moon has a star in front of it and apparently conveys the same message as the crescent moon itself. The star as we shall see below is no more than a chevron configured in a special way.

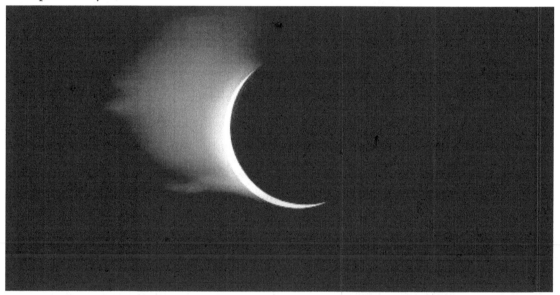

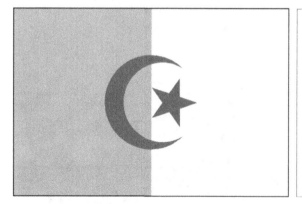

b) Interlocking circles

These are a variation of the circle. In fact, one can undo the interlocking circle and end up with one circle. The decorative symbol is found on Tonga wooden doors. It has also been found on the Ngoma Lungundu drum associated with the VaRemba/AbaLemba found in Mberengwa and also among the VhaVenda in the Limpopo Province of South Africa. In Zimbabwe the decorative symbol is found on the lapels of senior police officers' uniforms. We understand the army uniform also used to carry the decorative symbol but was discarded when it was viewed as a colonial symbol. Apparently, this is an African decorative symbol that long predates the arrival of colonizers in Africa and Zimbabwe in particular. The decorative symbol expresses African cosmology, and more specifically the idea of continuity, eternity, endlessness and infinity. The interlocking circles, like conventional circles, have no beginning and no end. The pdf symbol is a good example of a twisted circle which, when unraveled, becomes a circle. Interlocking circles have no beginning and no end. They depict endless movement and thus symbolize continuity, eternity, infinity and immortality.

Yoruba and Venda motifs (L) Ngoma Lungundu (R).

2c Broken concentric circles (*ibhayisikili*)

This is a favourite decorative symbol for the Ndebele women basket makers. Marjorie Locke (1996) interpreted the decorative symbol as a bicycle tyre pattern. Indeed, there are tyres that have track marks that look just like the decorative symbol in question. A lady who used to work at the Lupane Women Centre in the Lupane District of Matabeleland North in Zimbabwe advised me that the symbol could not have been inspired by the designs on a bicycle tyre. Some designs on the Ndebele ilala baskets were said to be representing leather skins, *amabhetshu* worn by Ndebele men. This was in reference to the triangles arranged back to back, what some people interpret as diamonds.

Broken circle design

When I visited Vancouver in Canada in 2002 I found mounted in one gallery an art exhibition which featured, inter alia, baskets of the First Nations (Red Indians) which had exactly the same "bicycle tyre designs" as those on Ndebele ilala baskets. Both the Ndebele and the Red Indians adopted their "bicycle tyre designs" long before the invention of the bicycle. The inspiration for and the adoption of the decorative symbol must have been the same, probably emanating from Africa. It is thought that the people of the First Nations left Africa and travelled to Asia and finally got to the Bering Strait that links Russia to Canada. At the time the strait was shallower than it is now and migrating people, people of the First Nations, got to what is now known as Alaska in Canada and streamed down till they got to the United States of America (USA) and further south to South America. The new arrivals brought with them visual traditions gleaned from Africa including the circular design, the coiling tradition of basket manufacture and indeed, the decorative symbols. We may not know the interpretation of the decorative symbol but at one point in time the symbol could very well have shared the same interpretation and therefore the meaning that was infused with common cosmology and design traditions. A decorative sugar basin that I purchased in England in 2014 exhibited the same design. The basket was from Rwanda.

After seeing the baskets of these First Nations women I remembered the lady from Lupane Women Centre and realized she was right not to pin down the interpretation of a decorative design to the Ndebele. The design was not to be pinned down to the Ndebele people whose nation came into being only recently. Even the Nguni from whom they are descended are equally a recent phenomenon that cannot be said to have inspired decorative symbols exclusively by themselves and for themselves. The underlying cosmologies, worldviews, axiology and aesthetics certainly predate both the Ndebele and the Nguni. What this means is that interpretations of decorative symbols cannot be pinned down to specific ethnic groups in Zimbabwe. The inspiration and adoption of the decorative symbols stems from a common cosmic inspiration adopted several centuries ago when the people were probably domiciled on the African continent, the cradle of humankind.

The *ibhayisikili* symbol consists essentially of parallel segments of circles which share a common centre that coincides with the centre of the coiled basket, which is where it starts, *isibhono*, the navel button. The parallel circles are joined to outer ones by vertical lines. We may not know what exactly inspired this particular decorative design other than to attribute it to observation of some cosmic phenomenon. We are thus able to decipher the meaning behind the decorative symbol. Concentric circles, broken or continuous, symbolize eternity, continuity, endlessness and infinity. It is important to see in the ilala basket reinforcement of the application of the circle namely: on the design of the basket itself, the coiling of ilala fibre around the cords, the 'circling' cords of grass (*umadodlwane*) and ilala fibre and the circular decorative symbols brought out through the use of brown dye from a tree called *umnyiyi*. We can surmise that the circle and the circular design were powerful expressions of the cosmology of the Ndebele people and indeed, other African peoples.

Coiled ilala basket from Canada (Campbell 1993)

3 The chevron decorative symbol

The first question that we should ask here is, "Does a chevron symbol exist in nature?" The answer is simple; the chevron decorative symbol does not exist in nature. It certainly dominates when it comes to the decoration of surfaces of artifacts. At that level and also on paper it exists as a two-dimensional (2D) representation of a three-dimensional (3D) reality. All along we have been referring to woman as the greater player in the effort of attaining continuity. Those who designed the chevron symbol knew something about human anatomy and human physiology. An intimate knowledge of biology and the application of attributes of African aesthetics and axiology informed the resulting symbol. At the level of biology the African knew that the part of woman that was involved in the attainment of continuity or fertility was that part of her that embraced the womb.

The boundary of the area in question is V-shaped, or a triangle. At the lower pointed end the tip is the sex organ. The two diverging ends are bounded by the pubic area and the thighs. However, the area extends upwards to include the button navel. The most critical body part within the defined area is the womb which apparently is circular in design. Note that the vagina's role is of secondary importance, merely the introduction of a man's sperms and as a birth canal. The womb on the other hand is where fertilization of the ovum (egg) takes place. The walls of the womb would have developed blood vessels to provide nourishment to the developing zygote and embryo. The embryo feeds through the placenta and gets rid of waste through the same blood system. The embryo is physically protected by the fluid contained in the amniotic membrane. The fluid is a shock absorber. The womb also protects the baby from both infra-red and ultra-violet radiation. This is just how the body of woman is adapted to deal with the natural process at the root of attainment of continuity. A lot of life-sustaining functions are carried out within and by the womb. The triangle or chevron unit embodies that part of woman.

Once the baby is born the body of woman is adapted physiologically to deal with the sustenance of the baby. This time, however, the baby suckles from mother's breasts till it is developed enough to be weaned off. Beyond weaning the human mother hands over to Mother Earth who continues to provide food to the growing child. The whole process is controlled by 'a chain of women.' A pregnant human mother is fed by Mother Earth. The embryo is fed by the human mother through the placenta and after birth the growing baby is fed by the human mother who in turn feeds on Mother Erath. A weaned baby feeds directly from Mother Earth. It is a cycle of mothers sustaining human life. The one mother, that is Mother Earth, is represented by a circle as already explained above. The human mother is this time represented by a chevron or triangle (a single unit of it)

However, when it comes to African aesthetics repetition comes in as it is a quality that lends beauty. A single chevron unit is repeated, or many of them are joined together thus imparting beauty to the rendition. Axiology also informs the final product. A woman's nudity is a serious violation of African ethics. A geometric symbol in the form of a chevron circumvents the problem. We find the same in the rock art of the San. Women were painted as images with breasts. Africa was less averse to men's exposure of their privates. This is borne by the fact that the San drew men with erect penises. It was their way of emphasizing the body part of men that played a part in sexual reproduction. A flaccid penis is no good in the attainment of continuity. An erect penis symbolizes success and in this particular case success in sexual reproduction and hence in the attainment of continuity. At the same time the erect penis could have been drawn to symbolize desired success in hunting. Success is not limited to just one human endeavour.

Even people who were not sure of what they were drawing included 'dots' or small shaded circles directly above the lower tip at the bottom of the chevron. To them the chevron is a snake, then the 'dots' become a problem which they have difficulty in handling. The angle of the chevron is given- determined by anatomy. Each person can use a compass to measure the angle of his/her own chevron unit in the privacy of their bedrooms or bathrooms. A snake, on account of its backbone, cannot execute that angle and survive. Certainly, as we mentioned above, a snake does bear the idea of continuity as it casts its old kin and acquires a new one. This is perceived as rebirth by Africans. The circular Uroboros or Ouroboros is a snake trying to bite its own tail. Continuity as enshrined through rebirth is inherent in a snake. Where a snake is represented, it is wavy as in water waves. The chevron symbol is certainly not representative of a snake. Africans knew human anatomy as distinct from snake anatomy and they were skilled artists able to execute what they perceived.

Why have we said the chevron does not exist in nature? If the body of woman is the inspiration behind the chevron symbol we should be aware that no woman is two-dimensional. If we look at the chevron symbol we get to realize that it is in reality a three-dimensional reality. No woman is two-dimensional. Instead, she is three-dimension. So what shape is that part of her which we represent on paper and crafts as chevron? The answer is simple-it is a cone with its apex facing down. A cone is, in reality, a circular symbol. Cut into an infinite number of circles it ends up with circles of increasing radii, if we start at the apex of the cone. If we however start at the top, where the cone is widest, we theoretically have an infinite number of circles of diminishing radii (plural for radius). So, we are really back to the circle, as the chevron is nothing but another form of a circle pregnant with the attributes that embody the idea of continuity and infinity as explained above.

The elements of African aesthetics that we alluded to are more apparent in the chevron decorative symbol: movement, repetition, rhythm (periodicity and regularity), symmetry, equilibrium and balance. Many African attributes, tenets and values are negotiated to arrive at the decorative symbol.

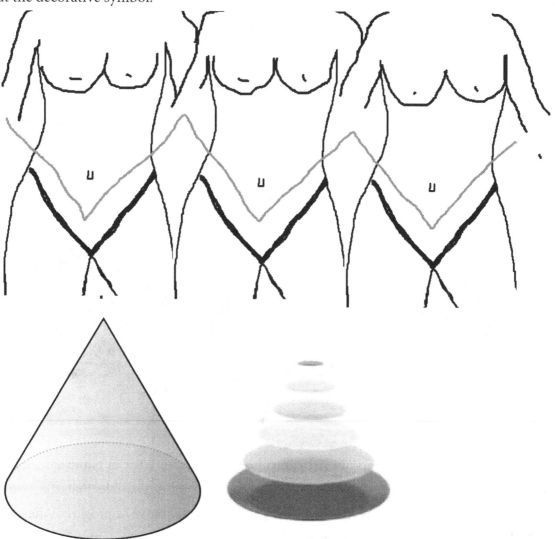

Variations of the chevron symbol

3a The star

When a decorative design manifests itself in various configurations sometimes we fail to see it as such. The chevron symbol, by virtue of its aesthetic appeal, has lent itself to various configurations. We do know that a star is circular in design, just like our own sun which is a star. However, the sun has been represented as a differently configured chevron generally referred to as the 'star'. Imagine a straight piece of paper with a chevron design-say five chevron units. The paper is placed on a flat surface. Pull the two ends towards each other till they meet. What you have now is a star with five units of the chevron. What we should appreciate here is that the star is in reality a differently configured chevron symbol. The meaning is still the same as interpreted above. In the cosmos the chevron does not exist. The circle which exists symbolizes the idea of continuity, endlessness and continuity. At the level of humans, the idea of continuity is symbolized by the body of woman, expressed as a chevron symbol. Besides, we have already indicated that a chevron in actual fact if a circle.

3b The triangle

The triangle, more specifically an isosceles triangle, is another representation of the open chevron. Pashapa (2009) says, "The chevron pattern is made by repetition with triangle. Therefore, there must be some relationship between the chevron pattern and the triangular windows on the huts, the three rows of clay pots in the kitchen, and the three stones on the fireplace and the first poles that are used in erecting the roof of a house(Pashapa 2009:16).

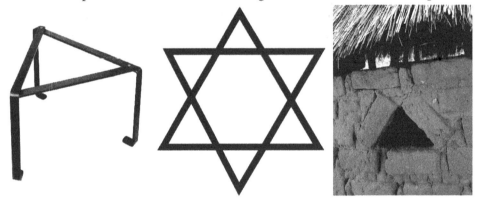

The figure three seems common in African cultural world. An African handshake has three elements to it. The triangle has three corners or ends. It is possible that the two ends represent male and female sex organs while the last is representative of progeny. Alternatively

the figure three is representative of male sex organs: two testes and one penis. The same applies to female sex organs. That would make the triangle a symbol of fertility and thus continuity. A fireplace has three stones. A cooking plate rests on the three stones and food cooks in the fireplace. Even the modern alternatives to the three hearthstones are made with a triangular shape. A pot rests on this metallic artifact. The triangular window on a kitchen wall is actually a chevron unit. Assuming this is the case, it makes sense to associate the 'figure three" with the idea of continuity. Instead of drawing the sexual organs, something that would go against the grain in terms of African moral ethics, the figure three is readily tolerated while at the same time symbolizing the sexual organs which render continuity possible in human beings and indeed other species of both the flora and fauna. The chevron itself can be said to have three ends although the two ends may not joined together. There does seem to be a bigger story than we have presented here with regard to the "figure three" and its manifestations in African cosmology and cultural practices. The Star of David is in reality two interlocking triangles. While the triangle symbolizes femininity or is a representation of woman and thus continuity, the triangle is sometimes used to depict masculinity, or the man depending on the direction that the apex is facing. If this be the case, the interlocking stars are symbolic of a natural process that results in procreation. In other words, the interlocking stars symbolize success and can be taken as a prayer for continued existence, which is the essence of eternity or infinity. The Jewish Sate , knowing the history of its creation would do well to pray for continued existence.

3c The cross

The cross is one symbol that has come to symbolize Christianity. Jesus Christ was nailed on the cross. What is important to realize though is that the cross predates Christianity. There are certain figures that are not easy to execute in practical terms. This problem has resulted in seemingly rectangular designs. The chess/checked board in one such. The cross is another. What we perceive as the aim in drawing a cross were four chevron units with their ends meeting at one common point. The Maltese cross is the more representative design to illustrate and represent the chevrons.

To link the nailing of Jesus Christ on the four chevrons seems to make sense in that he dies on the cross (read chevrons). All along we have been arguing that there is a close link between life and death. In fact, eternal life is unthinkable in the absence of death. By dying for three days Jesus Christ earned eternal life or continuity vested in the four chevrons. Death through crucifixion is followed by rebirth, the resurrection which translates to eternal life, the very essence of continuity.

We can look at the relationship between life and death at another level. Are we not sustained by death? We certainly eat death. We eat boiled (read killed) vegetables, eat fried or boiled eggs (read killed). It will become apparent that what we eat as food has been killed. Don't we slaughter cattle, chickens, sheep, goats and various other creatures before we eat them? Our lives, including those of plants, are sustained by death. In African terms death marks the end of flesh-spirit existence. The flesh is interred and the spirit enters the spiritual realm where it attains eternal life. Death unlocks eternal life by removing the death prone flesh, leaving that component with the attribute for eternal life.

3d Copper ingots at Great Zimbabwe

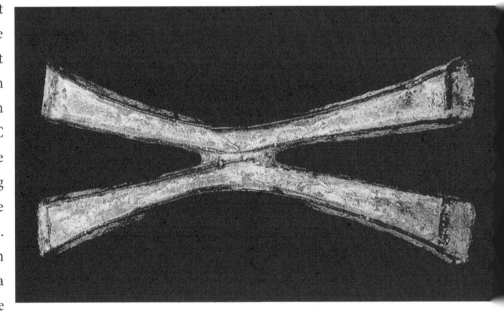

During excavations at Great Zimbabwe some copper ingots thought to have emanated from the copper belt in Zambia and the DRC were retrieved. We cannot help seeing some significance in the design of the ingots. Surely the easiest design to come up with was a rectangular one. The right angle though would have been in contradiction with the attributes of African aesthetics. A copper miner's prayer would be the exploitation of sustainable ores so that mining activity itself is sustainable. The benefits accruing from the trade in copper are sustainable. Would it then not make sense for an African miner to come up with a design of ingot that expresses the traits that we have alluded to above, traits that symbolize continuity in or sustainable mining? It would thus be proper to view the ingot in that perspective- the execution of two chevrons serving the same role as the cross. The chevrons are arranged tip to tip or apex to apex. It is just a matter of perception, Afrcan perception to be more precise! Anyway, what must be appreciated and never avoided is to make an attempt at interpreting the designs from an Afro-centric perspective-provided that we are agreed that the ingot is the work of an African mind.

Finally, let us point out that the chevron or its triangular version can be configured in several ways. Where two triangles are back to back some people have interpreted these as diamonds symbolized. When did the African start dealing in diamonds? When the African, at least the one in southern Africa, began working gold, he did not attach exchange value to it. Hitherto, he had been producing egg shell beads which were later replaced by glass beads traded from the East Coast. Gold was turned into beads, tjuma, meaning wealth and hence cattle, *n'ombe* in Tjikalanga. No wonder Tjuma/Tshuma people in Matabeleland are referred to as Golide. Singer Lovemore Majayivana Tshuma prides himself as Golide. Indeed, many Tshuma people cannot explain how they ended up with the praise name of Golide.

The multiplicity of chevron configuration on fabric is common, so it is on the baskets, clay pots and other artifacts. Hatchings are no more that chevrons with a "diamond" appearance. We can conclude this section by saying the chevron, in its various configurations and manifestations is stunningly aesthetic. It is even more stunning and exquisite when colour is added to the chevron designs.

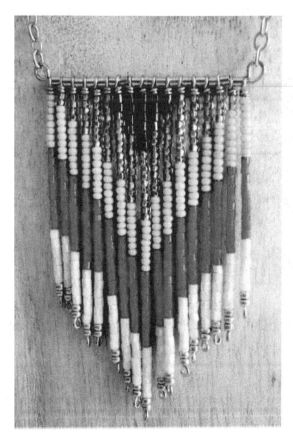 

3e Herringbone

Herringbone designs on Tonga baskets

This is a good example of a symbol executed to give variety. What will be pretty obvious is that the herring bone symbol uses a clear single unit which is the chevron. The difference here is how repetition was executed. In cases that we have cited above the units were repeated in such a way that the top ends of the V-shape were joined thus producing a longitudinally repeated V unit. This is not the case with regard to the herring bone. Instead, the Vs are packed, with one chevron unit pushed into another-all arranged along a stone wall. In the Zimbabwe type stone walls the herring bone, getting its name from a fish called a herring whose spine consists of bones arranged in a packing order. In the stone walls the herring bone decorative symbol is oriented along the horizontal stone courses.

The Tonga baskets also feature the herring bone decorative symbol. In terms of meaning the herringbone is no different from the chevron. The latter has a single V unit but aesthetic considerations have it repeated for maximum aesthetic effect. Similarly, the herring bone has

68

a single V unit of the same angle as the chevron. With both decorative symbols being inspired by the same anatomy of woman, we rightly expect them to have the same acute angle. Once again, the single V unit is repeated for maximum aesthetic effect. Overall therefore, the two decorative symbols are, in essence, representations of the same symbol with differing configurations.

The other comparison between the two is that both are inspired by faunal specimens. The more familiar chevron, in terms of its configuration, is inspired by the body of woman. The herring bone on the other hand, is inspired by the arrangement of the bones of a fish known as a herring. Perhaps what is the critical observation is the fact that the two chosen decorative symbols are inspired by nature. This is certainly not unique to the two decorative symbols. The circle as we saw is inspired by nature too. However, this time nature is represented by the design of the stars, planets and moons. Essentially, these are natural bodies that the Africans gleaned from long distances. The herring bone and chevron designs are inspired by nature as found on Mother Earth, closer home. Design inspirations came from near and far. The other variations of the chevron are inspired by the same natural phenomena, be it the cross, copper ingot or the star. Each one of them still carries the basic V as defined by the zone within a woman's body which embraces the all important womb where procreation is facilitated and continuity effected.

3f The chess/checked board

The chess board gets its name from a game of chess which has alternating squares of black and white. Other contrasting colours may also be used. The arrangement of the boxes in subsequent lines is such that no two similar boxes come one after the other; instead they alternate. Women in

Matobo District have produced stepped patterns on the walls of their huts during competitions under My Beautiful Home-Comba Indlu Ngobuciko. The one observation one quickly makes is that there are 90 degree angles whereas we have said Africans did not embrace rectangles in their architecture or art. One only needs to tilt one's head to see the hidden chevron. Practical considerations lead to the execution of seeming right angles. If the chevrons were accurately produced the angles would not be right angles but the ones that are dictated by human anatomy which informs the chevron.

We have seen similar 'squares' on the floors of Mater Dei Hospital in Bulawayo. However, as if to underscore that the 'squares' are not, in the true sense of the word, squares, they are not arranged in a a horizontal way that creates an impression that each box is a square. As a matter of fact, the 'square' is two triangles positioned back to back without their dividing bases. It is all about altering the configurations of the chevron to give the much sought after variety.

If we then move to the chess board we need to locate it on the surfaces where it is executed. The chessboard occurs on Zimbabwe type stone walls alongside chevrons, herring bones and dentelle. Admittedly, rock is not easy to work. The chess board is produced through leaving sunken 'squares' which are deeper than the surface of the walls. The sunken squares are so arranged that they alternate with higher surfaces. As a result, a chess board appearance is created on the wall through the construction technique. Two rows of the chess board are generally what are found on the stone walls. It is the 'sunken squares' that account for the creation of the chess board. As in the example given above, the seeming 'square' is two triangles back to back without their bases. The bases are imaginary. Eyes of the mind see the two triangles and their bases. Triangles so arranged do create an impression that there are right angles. It's really an optical illusion or a reality borne of practical considerations deriving from difficulty associated with working rock. Let us not lose sight of the fact that the surfaces of rock blocks are all that is chiseled and cut into the required shape which makes a façade of stone bricks. The very thick walls are filled up with roughly hewn stones. Only the faces, or facades, both inside and outside are finely hewn and give the impression of stone bricks.

What we are faced with then are the numerous decorative symbols on the stone walls all carrying the same meaning. It is just a question of effecting variations with the idea being expressed remaining the same-that of continuity. This should not come as a surprise as the decorative symbols are on walls of royal settlements. The rulers, without doubt, sought continuity of their own rule initially at individual level and then at the level of the lineage (continuity through succession within the lineage). With the king symbolizing the nation and its people, continuity at the level of rulers imparted continuity to the level of the nation. We only need to look at the burial practices of the Ndebele people. When a chief or ordinary person died he had his qualifying son hold a spear in front of the deceased father. Whereas the chief's sitting position signified the end of his era, the standing son expressed continuity of the lineage by taking over the father's position as chief of the community. Further, the spear was held with its blade piercing the ground.

There is more symbolism here than meets the eye. The spear should be perceived as a phallic object. The phallic object is being driven into Mother Earth. In other words the sexual act is being symbolized. This is being done in relation to the particular ruling dynasty. Sexual reproduction results in continuity. Here the line of the man who has fallen is being raised and extended into the future, something that is done in perpetuity. The spear shaft, *uluthi*, was broken and the metal blade carefully concealed somewhere. Twelve months later during *umbuyiso*, the bringing home of the spirit of the dear departed a new shaft was provided and joined with the metallic part. The spear was once again restored (Nyathi 2002) All this symbolized succession, or the continuation of the lineage, in this case vertically. The regenerated spear symbolized the regenerated or reborn chieftainship line. It all boiled down to continuity of the rule of the lineage-from father to son ad infinitum.

Let us take the image of the spear further. Among both the Ndebele and Bakalanga peoples when rain was accompanied by thunder, wind and lightning one person took a spear or axe and struck it into the ground and left it there-inserted. After the presentation on symbolic succession it should be easy to decipher the message carried on the cultural practice. The axe or spear clearly represents the phallic object, the male sex organ. The earth into which the axe or spear has been driven represents woman, Mother Earth, the female counterpart of the male. Africans believed a sexually starved woman was akin to a raging tempestuous storm. The storm was pacified in the same manner a woman was pacified and, pleased; by rendering her conjugal rights! Indeed the storm quietened. Peace be still

In some communities the king was seen as divine and a lot of reverence attended him. For example, the Ndebele monarch was hailed with the laudatory chant of 'Bayethe!' Those approaching him crawled on their fours, meanwhile shouting the praises of the king who had the power of life and death in his hands. The king did not directly address those coming to commiserate with him. He addressed the guests through his chief of chiefs, induna yezinduna.

Among the Balozwi the king faced away from the people that he was addressing. Familiarity breeds contempt. The king maintained his distance and thus his respect, awe and dignity. The Lozwi king had his dwellings surrounded by stone walls replete with the decorative symbols all of which were prayers that his rule be continued into eternity Stone lends strength and eternity as a result of relative resistance to elements that cause weathering. Clearly, if the king epitomized the nation he had to be well protected, both physically and metaphysically. Continuity implied the person of king being protected and after his death his line also being protected. The imposing and impregnable stone walls offered security to the king. Where the walls did not exist, the natural barriers such as sheer rock surfaces and cliffs provided the necessary physical protection. There are such cases both at Khami and Great Zimbabwe where, in the case of the latter, stone walls embrace huge rock boulders. Indeed, the king did express his socio-economic and political status through the imposing stone walls. Likewise, the stone walls fulfilled more than one function; they provided defence and that is pretty obvious. The limiting access, where people getting to the royal residence had to walk in a single file, was deliberately calculated to disarm would- be attackers. People approaching a royal residence in a single file are weaker than an army which approaches from all directions and attacking simultaneously. Where invaders are approaching in a single file the defending forces are better able to defend the royal settlement. Again this is the case both at Khami and Great Zimbabwe. To posit that the walls did not have a defensive function is to deny the beauty and protection provided by a presidential limousine. Such a car provides aesthetics, protection and mobility.

3g The dentelle

Crocodile with both Chevron and Dentelle designs.

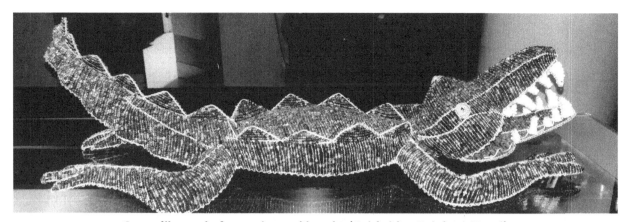

Crocodile made from wire and beads. (Beitbridge Rainbow Hotel)

This is another decorative symbol structurally executed on Zimbabwe tradition stone walls associated with royal settlements. Royalty was preoccupied with ensuring its continued hold on to power. At the individual ruler's level, he sought to stay in power till his demise-dying in office. Succession took place only after the death of the incumbent. At dynastic level the ruling lineage ensured that only members of the lineage ascended to the throne. If the ruling dynasty was Nembire of the Shoko totem, those taking over had to belong to the Nembire Shoko Vhudzijena dynasty. Where succession was lateral the various alternating "houses" all belonged to the lineage, all sharing a common totem, say Shoko. The perpetuation of one dynasty translates to continuity. The idea was expressed through artistic renditions executed on stone. Stone itself was expressive; it expressed, by virtue of its resistance to weathering, solidity and existence into eternity. Let us be alert to the idea that the type of succession is not the fundamental issue. Among the Ndebele people chieftainship succession was vertical. Of course there were instances when a line was terminated such as when a chief failed to produce sons, but instead produced girls only-*amawabayi* as they were called. In such a case there was lateral succession. Among the Shona there is lateral succession, the rotation of houses. What is important and common to both ethnic groups is that the chieftainship was retained within the lineage. A chieftainship belonged to a particular lineage. A Mafu chieftainship was earned by Mahubo(later known as Dambisamahubo as a result of his military exploits) who passed the baton to Mthikana, who in turn passed it on to Maduna then to Jim and then to Vezi the incumbent Chief Maduna of uGodlwayo. There were well known principles of succession and all sought to perpetuate the line within the descendants of the original chief who earned the right to rule over a given community.

As we have already seen above, the various decorative symbols on the stone walls are metaphors for women who contribute more than men towards ensuring continuity, endlessness, infinity and eternity, of the human species through sexual reproduction. It is these traits resident in women that the rulers desire- keeping the royal crown within the lineage or dynasty. The decorative symbols were thus a spiritual appeal to the ancestors to lend support in keeping the royal crown within the dynasty. It was a prayer executed through decorative symbols.

It comes as no wonder therefore to see all the decorative symbols carrying the same message or prayer. It has been observed that some male rulers kept their sisters within the royal settlements and sometimes committed incest with them. This was a realization by the rulers of the fact that women were the more important sex in the realization of continuity. What this then entails is that femininity was expressed through the circular design of the settlement and the decorative symbols, namely the dentelle, chess board, herring bone and chevron. In addition to these artistic renditions a woman, a sister, was used to reinforce and buttress the same idea. It had to be a sister who already belonged to the ruling dynasty. The aim was to retain the rule within the dynasty and which woman would achieve this more than a sister who already belongs. Sexual reproduction is what is symbolized in guaranteeing continuity. The biological act was thus performed with a blood sister with both partners belonging to the same lineage.

Let us now look at the decorative symbol referred to as the dentelle and see what exactly, within its design, expresses femininity which is behind continuity. Dressed stone bricks are arranged in the stone walls in such a manner that they are not in sync with the horizontal courses. Instead, one of the dressed angles in the stone is arranged so that it protrudes or juts out of the wall by a few centimeters. Let us for now deal with just one dressed stone brick. To the one viewing the wall he/she will see a chevron unit that stands out of the wall. Once again, we are back to the chevron unit that symbolizes a part of a woman's body. From the stand point of African aesthetics a single "V" or open triangle does not make an aesthetic impression. As a result, the architects aligned the protruding chevrons, each on one course the course below. To the viewer what is clear is a vertical arrangement of the chevrons. This looks more beautiful and that beauty has been effected through the application of one trait of African aesthetic, namely repetition. Whereas the herring bone and the chevron were aligned horizontally along the courses of stone walls, the dentelle is vertically arranged at right angles to the vertical stone wall.

We should appreciate that repetition has been applied in the arrangement of ALL decorative symbols be they chevron, dentelle, chess board or cord. The more familiar arrangement of the chevrons is what we see on the Royal Enclosure at Great Zimbabwe and other stone wall settlements. Each chevron unit is arranged horizontally within a course. There could be one more above or below with the same horizontal arrangement. In the herring bone the "V" or individual chevron units are arranged or packed with each base going into that of another. The emerging pattern is that of fish spine or herring bone. The dentelle has the same chevron units arranged vertically and protruding out of the stone wall. Variety is the spice of life. This is a case of re-arranging the same design that bears the same message. The message is one of continuity as expressed through feminine portrayal.

Professor Thomas Huffman (1996) sees the dentelle as representing the dorsal scales of a crocodile. He is perfectly right to see that. He may not have seen the part of woman's body which is rendered as a chevron. However, the crocodile is a chevron animal. In fact, reptiles are chevron animals in the manner in which their body components are arranged or aligned. The crocodile is the most "chevronic" of them. We need to see on a crocodile several chevron units: the dorsal scales (seen by Professor Thomas Huffman); the closed mouth, the open mouth with two chevron units; the angles on its legs, the chevrons between its toes and the "chevronic" tail. In other words, the African saw the crocodile as expressing continuity, by virtue of its myriad of chevron units which are repeated many times in many of its body parts. The chevron is rendered through its anatomy. Its chevrons resemble, in shape, the chevron within the body of woman which houses the womb, the organ most associated with procreation and thus continuity. The crocodile can thus easily replace woman in expressing the idea of continuity. The VaPfumbi that we referred to above were making use of this chevronic property of the crocodile in the succession rituals involving a stone retrieved from the late chief's decaying body, the stone that once was lodged in the stomach of a crocodile. The stone acquired the trait of continuity characteristic of the crocodile. Further, the stone which once resided in the stomach of a crocodile, *ingwenya/ngwena,* is restricted to the Ngwenya descendants who qualify as successors. This is a case where chieftainship is confined to one dynasty and continuity is effected symbolically.

In this regard is it surprising that the crocodile is featured on the pedestals of Zimbabwe birds? Their presence buttressed and reinforced a refrain of the same idea expressed by the decorative symbols given above. It is in the same vein that the VaPfumbi who are Ngwenya/Ngwena/BaKwena who are totemic crocodiles and chose a stone originally extracted from the stomach of a crocodile to ensure continuity as expressed through the succession ritual. Through association the stone has acquired the very important characteristic resident in the crocodile-namely continuity. Likewise, their chiefly rule is perpetuated by the symbolic stone that they extract from a decomposed body of the late chief to administer to the next chief. Succession is political continuity; from one member of the dynasty to the next regardless of whether it is lateral or vertical.

4 The phallic objects.

We have already made reference to axiology as one factor that conditions the final outcome of a symbol. Morality was an important screening consideration. We have observed the San drawing erect penises in their rock art and tried to explain the significance of erection or virility. While springing from sexual intercourse we should not lose cognizance of the fact that virility within the sexual sphere was taken beyond the particular into the general realm-a wish or prayer for success in a chosen endeavour. Virility or success in one realm translated to virility or success in another realm. Be that as it may, what is important for now is that the erect penis was not detailed for example as to show the glans. The two testicles are not apparent. It's the position of the 'rod' in relation to the body that expresses the idea of erection which is symbolic of the possibility of procreation and hence continuity. The final object detail has been tempered by considerations of morality. Here the penis is at a right angle to the body-in case of maximum erection.

Apparently this is not the case with female sexual organs. These were more revered and were not to be exposed in life nor were they to be exposed in artistic renditions, including visual traditions. This was not true of the San hunter-gatherers only but even their successors, the Bantu. There was indeed a lot of commonality in terms of cosmology, aesthetics and axiology between the Stone Age San and the Iron Age Bantu. Both were an African people, a people whose commonality is not rooted in the colour of their skins but in their worldviews. There has been some noticeable similarity between the San and the Ndebele and other people regarding the cultural practices and attended beliefs surrounding the eland. There was something special about this big antelope. When it was killed certain rituals were performed to "pacify" it beyond its demise.

The San were decorous enough not to draw female sexual organs. To visually indicate femininity they drew a woman's breasts. Both the breasts and the female genitals occurred together. Here our concern is not about expressions of womanhood. That has been dealt with. Our concern is with the expressions of fatherhood within the limitations set by considerations of African moral ethics. Africa knew that it took two to tango. While we have been harping on the bigger role played by the womenfolk in bringing about continuity, the men did play their own albeit secondary role in the natural game of procreation and hence continuity. Men's role would not have escaped visual representation.

Let us start with an incident we experienced at Amagugu International Heritage Centre (AIHC) a few years ago. There was an old lady, MaNyathi who was demonstrating the moulding of clay pots. One day she led Misheck Fobe Dube the senior guide and I to a place where she obtained clay. What is important to remember here is that Mother Earth if female and is fertilized by a male counterpart. The making of clay pots is at the human level equated to procreation. The two equivalent words in SiNdebele are the same, *ukubumba*, literally to create, build or procreate. Interestingly, the two processes are comparable in the manner they are attended to. Both are carried out in privacy, in normal circumstances. At the realm of human beings the two sides are pretty obvious. Here we shall deal with what MaNyathi asked Dube and me to do to work out the female side of the procreative equation. Before we got to the site where clay was to be excavated, MaNyathi asked us each to pick up one piece of wood. We obligingly did as commanded and she then asked us to throw down "our pieces." That was all that was required of us and MaNyathi proceeded to excavate the clay. Apparently, we had bought our right to participate in all the processes of pottery making.

The question is,"What was the significance of the wooden pieces that we were asked to pick up?" We have said before to understand the African of yesteryear we need to appreciate among other things, symbolism. To the traditional African symbolism was as real as the sun that rises to the east and sets in the west. Mother Earth was about to be injured, by MaNyathi. Pain was about to be inflicted on her though excavation. In order to ease her pain and add some dimension of sustainability in clay excavation, the male sexual(symbolized by the wooden pieces we picked up)organ was introduced which endeared us to grieving Mother Earth. In the absence of having performed the ritual, we would have been excluded from clay excavation, potting and the firing of same. We would have been totally excluded from all stages in clay pot making. Indeed, as MaNyathi went about her business, she excluded all other men who had not taken part in the ritual.

We were attached in a symbolic manner to Mother Earth and she would not exclude us. Through our pieces were paid for access. The pieces of wood remember are cylindrical. Remember too that our sexual organs are cylindrical. MaNyathi did not have to know the underlying symbolism. She operated a.t the literal level through the carrying out of cultural practices without any link to the cosmological underpinnings. This is apparently the case with other cultural practices. They are regarded at face value without due attention to what informs them, the philosophical grounding.

So what did our cylindrical pieces do to Mother Earth? They sweetened her out of her pain and pacified her. There was copulation that the ritual symbolized and ended with symbolized joy and ecstasy. MaNyathi could now proceed to extract clay while Mother Earth remained sedated, as it were. This may sound somewhat pornographic. But, are we not products of confined pornography? This is the extent to which Africa engaged symbolism to facilitate desired outcomes. There was constant interplay in terms of metaphor between the human body and its operations and the natural world. Dual manipulation went in both directions.

More specifically, at the level of continuity male and female symbols were used to bring about success or the desired state. Sexual reproduction was by and large assured of success, success in effecting continuity. That imagery was used with maximum effect where a given endeavour was to succeed. This included perpetuating a chiefly lineage, planting seed and in settlements such as Great Zimbabwe. At Great Zimbabwe phallic objects were recovered. However, the recovered artifacts operated at the educational level as teaching aids during lessons attending the ceremonies of girls who reached puberty. The colossal structures, largely female on account of their being circular, would have required bigger structures to counterbalance the female factor. When it is suggested, by Aeneas Chigwedere(2014), that the conical tower is a gigantic phallus that matches a gigantic woman (Royal Enclosure) we need to at least pay attention.

Male sexual organs are "elongated packed circles" or cylinders and are symbolized by such images. The circle (female) and the cylindrical object (male) are the visual metaphors that have been used in Africa to convey the idea of sexual reproduction and the attainment of continuity. These images have taken the shape of dolerite stone bands at Great Zimbabwe and other stone settlements in Zimbabwe and the larger region (South Africa, Botswana and Mozambique). In Egypt the burial places of the pharaohs had pyramidal writings that included the Ankh, comprising rod(read cylinder, the male component) and an attached circle(female organ).

A look at the flags of Zimbabwe, Mozambique, Palestine and South Africa will reveal the same arrangement: bands that seem to go into the tips of triangles. Remember the triangle or chevron is female, it being inspired by the body of woman. Anatomically, the tip is here a metaphor of the vagina. The intruding band is thus symbolic of a male sexual organ engaging woman in a sexual act-in the act of procreation and thus continuity. It turns out all the countries cited above engaged in protracted armed liberation struggles. The idea of sustainable wars is here being symbolized. Interestingly, the designers of the flags did not see the significance and symbolism of the images that they designed.

The Ankh, a part of the Egyptian pyramid writings comprised a circle (female sex organ) and a rod (male sex organ) brought together by a short rod between them. The Ankh has also been referred to as the knot of life and was used by the Khoi-San people for healing. It has also been called the key of life or a cross with a handle. It represented mythical eternal life. The Ankh represents rebirth through the life-giving power of the sun. Within the pyramid where the Pharaoh's corpse was interred the Ankh gave life to the departing spirit and guided it into another life in another realm, the spiritual realm. The Khoi-San, an African people regarded the same symbol as giving life of healing. Is this not indicative of common cosmology between the Egyptians and the Khoi-San? The Egyptians in question have been in Africa from a long time ago and not the present Arabs who are recent arrivals in Egypt.

Pestle and mortar.

Recently, I was looking at the BaTonga women's smoking pipe and I could not help seeing the sexual act symbolized through the belly (rounded and so female) of the smoking device and the pipe (cylindrical and so male). Sexual intercourse is two circles, one circular the other modified circles to attain a cylindrical form with piercing power, engaging each other. A walking stick comprising a circle at the top (handle) and a long cylinder makes interesting observation in this African rendition of sexual intercourse and the conveyance of the idea of continuity.

Fire place (L) The Ankh (R)

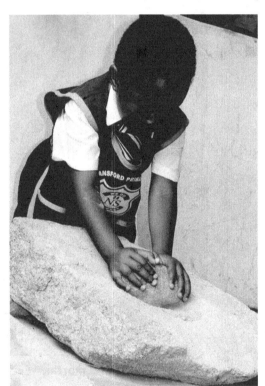
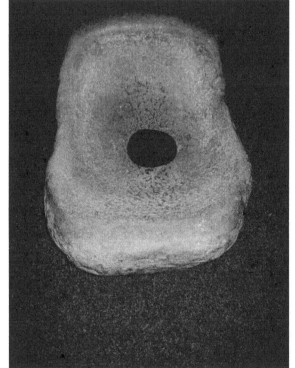

Pupil from Newmanford Primary School, Bulawayo using a grinding stone.

6 Spiral

The spiral, among the Shona people of Zimbabwe, is represented by the conus shell disc, *ndoro*, which used to be worn by the chiefs, as a necklace hanging from their chests."The first item of royal insignia to grace the new Chief was the NDORO, the conus shell disc. No chief was deemed to be a chief without the NDORO, the royal emblem (Chigwedere 2014:20). Chigwedere points out that some chiefs wore even four conus shell discs to express their greatness. "The important thing is that the chief had been graced with the royal emblem-the NDORO. The NDORO does not rot and can survive for decades. For this reason, the particular NDORO used to grace Chief Nembire could be the original NDORO used by his founding father. If so, this becomes another source of divine inspiration (Chigwedere 2014:21).

Chigwedere does see the idea of continuity that is expressed through the use of the ndoro. He attributes the expression of the idea to the fact that the ndoro does not rot and can last for decades. While the ndoro is certainly hard and dry thus making it resistant to decay, it is another trait that the Shona, who shared a common cosmology and worldview with the rest of Africa, identified in the ndoro. There are many other snails with shells that do not decay and can last long. They were not chosen because they did not have the quality or trait found on the ndoro-its spiral shape. In fact, when the ndoro is being prepared for royal use, it is only a part of it, that which has a spiral that is made use of. The rest is discarded. One could say it is the rear part of the conus shell that is used.

Chigwedere brings in another important dimension-that of passing the conus shell disc from one chief to the next, probably beginning with the founding chief. This is, in actual fact, the expression of continuity which is structurally expressed by the spiral design. As a matter of fact, the ndoro with its spiral design and the chevron constitutes the beaded part of the chief's ngundu, the royal ostrich hat express the same idea; continuity extending from the past to the present and into the future. For the Ndebele with vertical descent the idea was clearly expressed, from father to son ad infinitum. Some African rulers, given a choice, would want to be succeeded by their own sons, thus perpetuating their dynasties in traditional African style. The idea of limited terms is anathema to some of them. They want to rule till they die in office. The best lesson for this has come from King Mzilikazi of the Ndebele people who said,"No sun rises before the other has set. There are never two suns in the same sky." The electoral process turns out to be a big farce as some leaders rig elections or harass and hound the opposition political parties to ensure they continue sitting on the throne and wearing the crown for eternity at personal level and then passing the baton from their graves to their succeeding sons. This is how Africa dealt the issue of succession within the context of divine chiefs and kings. Continuity of rule is what Africa knew and the idea is expressed by, for example, the wearing of ndoro by chiefs and the use of the chevron decorative symbol on royal settlements such as Great Zimbabwe, Khami, Naletale and others.

Let us now turn to the ndoro, the conus shell disc with a spiral and see how it expresses the idea of infinity, continuity, endlessness and eternity the very values that a modern African leader wishes to embrace., more so when the leader is surrounded by leaders who are hereditary and are not elected: the village heads, headmen and chiefs. This is the bifurcated state that Mahmood Mamdani referred to. Essentially, the conus are a circular design. It differs from a circle in that it has a clear beginning but it spirals out into theoretical eternity. While it clearly has a beginning, it has no end. Theoretically it will embrace the entire universal space. Its movement has no end. The rule of one incumbent may end, but at dynastic level it recreates itself through succession through the ruler's eldest son. The conus shell, being a spiral, signifies eternity. It expresses the burgeoning universe which continues to expand outwardly even today-though it might have had some beginning in the distant past. When an Ndebele woman coils an ilala fibre round a cord of grass, made from *umadodlwane* she is expressing eternity. At the same time, the basket cord is spiraling. The double spiraling-at right angles to each other reinforce the idea of continuity and eternity. In fact what is there is eternal spiraling. The Tonga baskets which are woven also bear the element of spiraling-moving in front and behind the slanting ilala shreds. The spiral embraces constant change which lends continuity. The spiral is thus a symbol for change, a sign for unity in that the burgeoning spirals are held together at source. The spirals stand in relation to source without which their existence is unimaginable. A spiral may be seen as an upward spiraling path through time, linking past present and future. Many objects bear the spiral: kudu horn, eland horn (said to be having a 'snake'), impala horn, galaxies, fingerprints, shells of snails, water whorls, whirlwinds and cyclones such as one that ravaged Fiji Island on 20 February 2016. The spiral, as a symbol that expresses birth-death and rebirth, is what made it the choice as an emblem that chiefs used to express continuity in the lineage of rulers, regardless of whether succession was lateral(as among the Shona) or vertical(as was/is the case among the Ndebele)

Spiral shape (L) Spiral on a basket (R) (Campbell, 1993)

Conus shell

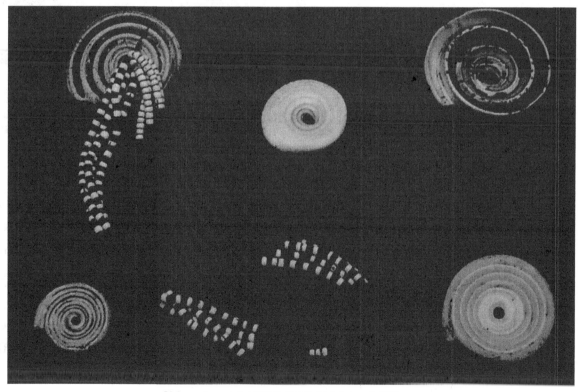

Ndoro from a conus shell (Mawere, 1997).

7 Whorl ('Umoya')

The whorl as a decorative symbol is mostly found on Ndebele coiling baskets. In the SiNdebele language they refer to this particular symbol as '*umoya*' meaning wind which is moving air. The spiral or coil as depicted above is different from this particular symbol whose 'arms' are curving and generally four in number. This is a vortex which captures the behaviour of moving fluids. Africans have generally not been regarded as people with a comprehensive knowledge of astronomy. The Africans of today have certainly retrogressed in terms of knowledge of astronomy that they possess. Colonization and the introduction of western education tended to give less credence to knowledge possessed by Africans. Even today such knowledge, not regarded as real knowledge, is termed indigenous knowledge as if there is knowledge which is not indigenous to a particular community. Some people have religions while Africans have African Traditional Religion (ATR). Just which religion is not traditional to its people?

Whorls on Ndebele and Tonga Baskets

The Dogon of Mali, an African people, have known about the Dog Star long before the telescopes from the Western world identified it. In their religious practices the Dogon have observed rituals that recognize the 65-year orbit of the Dog Star. What is true is that Africans wil,l in their visual art expressions, depict something they may not know about. Some dances may express deep cosmic knowledge but the dancers do not necessarily know about what they are expressing. It is the same with the use of decorative symbols. Ndebele women will not tell much beyond 'umoya theory' about what is expressed by the whorl they execute through brown dye on their coiling baskets. Even as they execute designs on their faces they will come up with cosmic reality that they know next to nothing about.

In actual fact what the women are expressing is the Milky Way which, in SiNdebele, is called *umthala*. The word refers to both the expansive Milky Way with its several galaxies and the part of the stomach that resembles where it has been stitched up, joined together. It is the thicker and finer portion of the stomach. Apparently, the solar system, within which the earth is found, is tucked away near one of the four 'arms'. The four arms do exist as found in visual artistic renditions of the 'umoya' decorative symbol. Through visual ar,t the women unknowingly capture and express lost knowledge of their ancestors relating to astronomy. What is knowledge and how is it gained? This is an epistemological question that should vex our minds.

Now that we know what 'umoya' symbol represents, we need to go further and identify its traits that make it relevant to the pervasive African theme, that of continuity. More that the spiral, the whorl graphically expresses movement, that burgeoning circular movement. Constant and rhythmic change is being expressed. The arms have a common source or origin which binds them together-making them relate to each other and to their source-a common source. The traits of a circle are apparent here and that means the interpretation applicable to the circle is equally applicable in this instance. Do we really know when the Milky Way originated? Are we not equally at a loss as to when the Milky Way will come to an end, if at all it will? Answers to both questions imply the omnipresent idea of continuity, eternity, infinity, endlessness and immortality.

The Milkyway

8 Cross hatchings

Cross hatchings are commonly found on the necks of clay pots made by women in several communities such as the Shona. Ceramic typologies have been used to glean a lot of information with regard to the movement of communities. Perhaps much more important than tracing the movements is to know the cosmologies that these people embraced and how they shared these with other peoples. This is possible because the clay pots bear both individual and community signatures that link them in terms of decorative symbols that they bear and the techniques and traditions of manufacture. Fired clay pots are durable and generally become a part of assemblages that archaeologists retrieve during their excavations of settlement sites. When ceramic typologies are matched, patterns begin to emerge such as the Kwale Ware on the eastern part of central and southern Africa. The assumption is that communities that share the same ceramic typologies share the same or related origins and did, at some time in their lives, share common traditions. Those common traditions are products of shared common worldviews, beliefs, aesthetics and cosmologies.

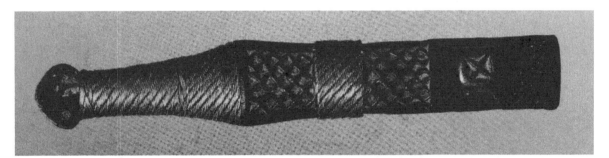

Scabbard with cross hatching. (Ellert, 2002)

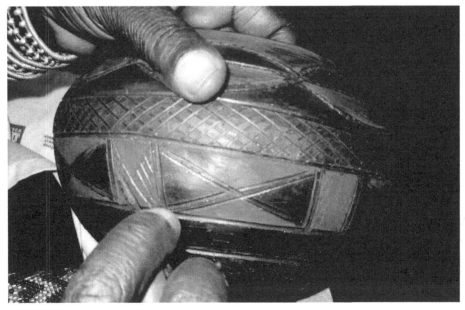

Claypot with cross hatching. (Ellert, 2002)

It is a pity though that basket typologies have not been used for the same purpose as ceramic typologies. It is recognized that baskets bear a wider range of decorative symbols than clay pots. As a result, the baskets would reveal more information in terms of African cosmologies and worldviews than what the clay pots provide. Which communities in north-east Africa, central and southern Africa make coiling baskets? Which communities make baskets through weaving? Are the communities that produce coiling baskets closer to each other than the communities that make their baskets through weaving? I have seen coilers in South Africa, Botswana, Swaziland, Malawi, Tanzania, Kenya, Somalia, Rwanda, Burundi and Ethiopia. These countries and their communities seem to occupy a certain part of the African continent. Variety in repetition engenders peace and tranquility to the mind. We saw his with the varied configurations of the chevron. In fact, the rendition of the same idea of continuity in various ways is part of rendering peace and solace to the mind.

Battle axe with cross hatchings. (Ellert 2002)

Triangles may be lying back to back, as if symbolic of diamonds and their strength. Hatchings are no more than crossing oblique lines. The lines are inclined at different angles and what are formed are 'diamonds' which in reality are two triangles back to back. What we need to perceive is that the triangles have unmarked bases. A lot of these back-to-back triangles result from the several oblique lines intersecting each other. There are clay pots with parallel

87

slanting or oblique lines that are not intersecting. Sharpened pieces of wood were used to inscribe or engrave the incised lines. The Ndebele potters used this mode of ceramic embellishment on the necks of their pots. Either the oblique lines all slanted in the same direction or in one part of the pot they slanted in one direction and in another section the direction of slant changed-thus creating some overall impression of 'unconnected chevrons' when the lines are extrapolated.

In essence the hatchings are a myriad of triangles or chevrons and their meanings are the same as those given above. All this may sound too simplistic and sme pedestrian over reliance on articulation of a monothematic idea. However, we arrive at this conclusion after many years of observation and study of African cultural practices and later seeking to unearth their cosmological underpinnings. It became apparent that Africans were indeed preoccupied with attaining continuity and even when they engaged in artistic endeavours, they still expressed that all pervasive idea of continuity. Only when we ask the question 'why?' in relation to the various cultural practices, are we in a position to perceive, unravel and unearth the underlying theme.

9 Oblique lines

Oblique incised lines have been observed on ceramics. As pointed out above sharp wooden sticks were used to imprint the shallow grooves while the clay was still wet, that is, soon after the potter made the clay pot. One could argue that a single oblique line could not effect the desired aesthetics. Repetition of the one oblique line fulfilled one attribute of African aesthetics namely, repetition. Visually, the resulting pattern captures the attention of the eye. It certainly is more riveting than just a single oblique line.

However, the question is whether this emerging pattern or just the single oblique line has some meaning at all. We may hazard a guess, but it must be conjecture that makes sense from an Afro-centric perspective. We shall turn to the dances to seek possible interpretation. It has been observed that there are communities whose dancers assume a vertical posture when dancing. This is particularly so of the Nguni (Ndebele, Zulu, Xhosa and Swazi) whose dances are expressions of their martial arts. Through their military prowess, they came to dominate other communities in the first quarter of the 19th Century. Standing upright expresses authority and overlordship. The master does not bow to his subordinates. Being erect is expressive of one's authority and conquering exploits. This domineering posture is extended to performances which, as a matter of fact, are cultural expressions. It also defines an individual's relationship to the physical environment. He is master over it-he will dance by stamping his authority over it, perform military movements including holding of spears, chanting and poetic renditions.

However, on most ceramic pots the lines are not vertical but oblique. These are embellishing traditions of communities that dance with their bodies in reverence to Mother Earth or some God such as Mwali of the Bakalanga. The most extreme example of this reverence is among the VhaVenda whose women lie on the ground to express reverence. The Wosana Dance of the Bakalanga/Banyubi people has the dancers performing in a stooping posture. Wosana is a rain-making dance performed at rain shrines such as Njelele in Matobo, Manyangwa in Bulilima District and Ntogwa in Ramakgwebana, in Botswana (Chikomo and Nyathi 2014). The communities had strong environmental conservation ideologies based on reverence of the environment and Mwali who resided in mountain

Venda women showing respect (kulocha)

caverns. One expects this reverence which is displayed as slanting lines to be captured beyond their performances. Indeed, the visual art traditions of the communities, who by the way are closely related to the Shona, bear slanting lines on their ceramics.

Reverence of the environment is practiced for a purpose. There is acknowledgement of human dependence on the environment. If the community is to survive into eternity it has to live in harmony and reverence of the environment. In the final analysis, what the community is seeking is the very idea of continuity. The environment was not revered or respected for the intrinsic value. Africa seeks functionality, utility benefits, at individual, group and community levels, in her pursuits. On ceramics of the same communities painted bands have been executed and these could symbolize the phallus, .that rendering of masculinity that completes the picture of procreation through sexual reproduction.

A look at the chevron symbol will indicate two lines that are oblique. These are the two lines that constitute the V shape. If one of these lines is used and repeated we end up with oblique lines. If the other line is used we also end up with oblique lines but slanting in the opposite direction. Let us also consider that the decorative symbols that we are here dealing with are executed on ceramics which are representative or symbolic of women. Women or femininity requires masculinity to balance the equation of life, the equation of continuity and eternity and endlessness. However if we consider that the line is in actual fact representing a 3D reality then it is possible the line is a phallic representation which then, being male, balances the equation: male and female resulting in procreation which, in humans, is at the centre of continuity.

Painted bands have been observed on walls where they are represented by soils mixed with different coloured pigments. The walls are circular and therefore represent the female element. To balance the equation and express the idea of continuity the bands may be seen as representing the male element. Practical considerations make the band go round the wall instead of it being at right angle to the wall. The BaTonga smoking pipe for women more appropriately approximates the relevant angle or orientation. How is a San hunter with an erect penis to have a similar theme executed on a hut wall, other than through a band that goes round the wall?

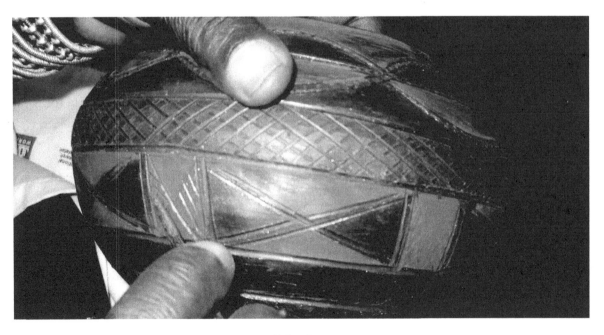

Zulu claypot.

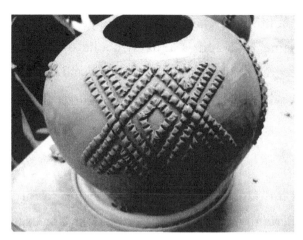 

Zulu clay pots (Delius 2007 (L))

10 Water waves

Water waves have smooth bends which differ markedly from the chevron whose angle is anatomically determined. Waves are smoother and come in rhythmic successions. Emanating from some point, they spread out and theoretically they will spread out indefinitely. In essence therefore, the waves represent energy .One wave in a vast pool of water will not cease to grow. There is thus no end to its advance. That way, it is similar to a whorl or a spiral. All the waves have an epicenter and radiate out of it, theoretically without end. It is this 'without end' attribute that led to the water waves being adopted as a decorative symbol to express continuity. In terms of execution this is a symbol that is markedly similar to a snake which also expresses the idea of continuity on account of its moulting. A new snake emerges from an old snake, a phenomenon akin to succession within a chieftainship. The Ndebele people of Zimbabwe say, *"inlathu ivuka emfukuleni wayo."* A python emerges from the backbone of a dead one. This is an expression of the idea of rebirth or regeneration and explains why the snake found its way into those symbols that express the idea of continuity, eternity, infinity, immortality and fertility. Traditional doctors wore vertebrae of a python for the very reason that a python emerges from a dead one in the same manner that the doctor makes use of power from a dead ancestor.

Besides, let's appreciate a certain quality of water which lends it to the expression of continuity. Water will exist in three states at normal temperatures. It occurs as a liquid which can be transformed into a gaseous form (water vapour or steam). The vapour may be condensed back into liquid water. Liquid water freezes into solid ice which may in turn be melted back into liquid water. This water cycle is akin to other natural cycles such as the setting and rising of the sun and the emergence of a new moon, its waxing and eventual 'death.' The dead moon rises and the cycle continues. This constant change is the basis of continuity in nature. Water displays the same trait and is thus symbolic of continuity. Africans did not fail to embrace water as a decorative symbol, some kind of visual language to express the idea of continuity; an idea also expressed in several other genres of communication.

11 Concluding remarks

We can only hope that this preliminary and introductory book will spur further research so that we begin to unravel Africa's identity. Certainly, a lot remains to be done, for example researching the decorative symbols of the rest of black Africa and establishing commonalities that should enable us to arrive at better informed generalizations and conclusions. By so doing we are opening ourselves up to echoes from the past, a past within which our heritage is embodied. Signals from the past are there for us to intercept and sample. The question is whether we have the receptors to receive the encoded messages and decode them for our consumption.

Sadly, when it comes to epistemology Africa is all the worse for abandoning her own ways of acquiring knowledge. Africa has swallowed hook line and sinker Western epistemological traditions. Anything African is trashed, demonized and denigrated. As a result, Africa has come to despise spirit mediumship which was, and still is, albeit at lower operational levels, a way of receiving echoes from the past. The very decorative symbols that we seem to be grappling with were developed by African ancestors who knew what meaning was carried by each symbol. Subsequently, in later years the aesthetic symbols and their meanings divorced. The ancestors knew the pre-divorce status as it was the time when they lived prior to transcending the material realm to continue leading eternal life in the spiritual realm. The ancestors in question continued to communicate with their progeny which was calculated to protect their progeny and ensure their welfare. Through the same spiritual phenomenon, Africa could foretell the future; foresee the weather, short term, medium term and long term. During the armed struggle spiritually, more specifically spirit mediumship was called upon to come to the assistance of the freedom fighters. The spirits such as those of Mbuya Nehanda had their support solicited during the liberation struggle but only to be abandoned at independence in favour of religions that had never been called upon to assist in the prosecution of the armed liberation struggle. Liberation heritage accounts from the operating foot soldiers abound with spiritual interventions. The sidelining of the ancestral spirits whose support had been solicited at the star of the struggle amounted to a monumental betrayal of our ancestors who to this day have not disarmed. No one ever told them that the war was over. More ungratefully they were never thanked for their role. Used and abused!

In academia mere mention of African Spirituality, especially as it relates to epistemology invokes classical derision, ridicule, mockery and scorn. Western scholarship calls the tune and dictates acceptable epistemologies. Oral traditions are said to be short-lived and can't be relied upon. Spirit mediumship regenerated itself in order to transmit information and knowledge from the distant past to living generations. Medicinal knowledge was transmitted in the same manner-but along chosen channels in the context of chosen spirit mediums. African rulers did keep within their royal residences traditional doctors and spiritual seers who performed various functions ranging from metaphysical protection of the royal elite to fortifying the royal residences.

Africa today no longer believes in these epistemologies and spiritual interventions. Alternative proselytizing religions have undermined African Spirituality. The result has been groping in palpable darkness and inventing and re-inventing Africans that fit the prejudicial and imperial mould. This, sadly, is perpetrated as if Africa does not have and has never had the capacity to access information and knowledge from her past. Sustained intellectual guessing and conjecture are deemed superior to resorting to ways of accessing knowledge that were in vogue long before conquest and subjugation. African ways are at best superstitious!

Decorative symbols offer us a development paradigm which is not linear. The circle, that cosmos-wide design posits a cyclical mode for development which grows, grows and gets more complex with neither limit nor end. But lo and behold, Western development paradigms are foisted on Africa, sometimes kicking and screaming and other times gleefully enjoying it. These are essentially linear paradigms that run counter to African values and principles. But Africa whimpers like a wounded and freezing dog that never sees itself as having a choice. Development has been reduced to fruitless catching up, a fallacious, misleading and erroneous pursuit which has not yielded any positive and sustainable paradigms of development. A people cannot be developed, as Tanzanian President Mwalimu Julius Nyerere used to say. Development is normative, defined in terms of the desired end state by the people themselves, applying methodologies and strategies meaningful and relevant to their total situation. African cosmologies should be given room to decide the ways Africa should follow. The desired end results of development can never be universal. Political and development paradigms stand to fail at tremendous cost to the dignity and respect for Africa. The decorative symbols do tell us we see and envision different goals on the basis of our understanding of interpersonal, intergroup, intercommunity and intersocietal relations on the one hand and relations of all of these to the wider environment, both physical and spiritual. When Africa is instructed which way or ways to follow, Africa gets nowhere! Africa gets terribly incapacitated and emasculated.

Any meaningful attempt at interpreting the decorative symbols should be grounded on a strong grasp and understanding of the broader ethnography of the people whose symbols are being interpreted. Even more important is to be deeply grounded in their cosmology as it provides the underpinnings for cultural practices, rituals and ceremonies. In fact, we can argue that it is cosmology and worldview that inform the designs and infusion of meanings and messages in decorative symbols. Seeing as we are here dealing with visual art traditions, African aesthetics has to be taken on board so as for us to identify the dictates that are attributable to it. Similarly, dealing with the visual arts requires us to be alert to the moral ethics of the community whose decorative symbols are being studied and interpreted. Finally, we have to respect and recognize the epistemological traditions of the people and their art traditions that are being studied. The least that should happen is to allow lenses tinted with prejudice, chauvinism, bigotry and racism to colour our interpretations.

Saki Mafundikwa says, "Afrika's problem is that we let others define our worth, we never see the value in ourselves and our work unless an outsider validates or praises us." He cites the cases of singer Paul Simon in the song 'Graceland' and Pablo Picasso the Italian artist who after coming into contact with African art began to lend credence to it and by so doing thrust it onto the world stage of universal art.

References/Bibliography

Asante, MK 1987 The Afrocentric Idea Temple University Press Philadelphia

Burrett, R and Hubbard, P 2015 Great Zimbabwe: Spirits, Stones and the Soul of a Nation Khami Press Bulawayo

Burrett, R and Hubbard, P 1990 The Matopo: A short History The Amalinda Collection Bulawayo

Campbell, D (ed.) Native American Art and Folklore: A Celebration Crescent Books Avenel NJ

Carton, B Laband, J and Sithole, J 2008 Zulu Identities: Being Zulu, Past and Present University of KwaZulu-Natal Scottsville.

Chigwedere, AS 2914 Shona Chieftainship: Principles of succession Mutapa Publishing Harare

Chigwedere, AS (nd) The Karanga Empire Books for Africa Harare

Chigwedere, AS 1982 Birth of Bantu Africa Books for Africa Harare

Chigwedere, AS 1980 From Mutapa to Rhodes: 1000-1890 A D

Chiwome, E, Furusa, M, Mberi, EN Masasire, A and Mutswairo, S 1996 Introduction to Shona Culture Juta Zimbabwe Eiffel Flats

Delius, P 2007 Mpumalanga: History and Heritage University of KwaZulu-Natal Press Scottsville

Dehnem, B Stepping Stone: Art Journeys Around the World: Cultures Art Religion Christian Aware Leicester

Dewey WJ and Palmnaer, ED 1997 Legacies of Stone: Past and Present Volume 1 Royal Museum for Central Africa Tervuren

Ellert, H 2002 The Traditional Art of Zimbabwe CBC Publishing Bath

Elliot, A 1989 The Ndebele Art and Culture Struik Publisher Pretoria

Freland, FX 2009 Capturing the Intangible: Perspectives on the Living Heritage United Nations Educational Scientific and Cultural Organization Paris

Gray CC 2001 Afrocentric Thought and Praxis: An Intellectual History Africa World Press Asmara

Gutsa, T 2012 Tapfuma Gutsa's Mulonga: Deep Waters and Starry Skies, A Celebration of Tonga Culture and Heritage Culture Fund of Zimbabwe Trust in partnership with Sida Harare

Hamilton. C (ed.) The Mfecane Aftermath: Reconstructive Debates in Southern African History University of Natal Press Scottsville Pietermaritzburg

Huffman, T 1996 Snakes and Crocodiles: Power and Symbolism in Ancient Zimbabwe Witwatersrand University Press Johannesburg

Jung, CG 1986 Woman's Mysteries: The Inner Life of Women Revealed in Religious Myth and Ritual Century Hutchinson Publishing Group Melbourne

Kerber Art 2015 Mawonero/Umbono: Inspiration on Art in Zimbabwe British Council

Kunzwana Women Association 2015 Ilala: Chilelema Village Basketry Binga

Locke, M 1994 The Dove's Footprints: Basketry Patterns in Matabeleland Baobab Books Harare

Mbiti, JS 1975 Introduction to African Religion Heinemann International Literature Oxford

Mbiti, J S 1970   African Religions and Philosophy Heinemann London

Murove, FM (ed.) African Ethics: An Introduction of Comparative and Applied Ethics University of KwaZulu-Natal Scottsville

National Art Gallery of Zimbabwe 2015 The Traditional Kitchen Design Zimbabwe

National Gallery of Zimbabwe 2014 Basket Case II

Ndlovu, A 2014 Zimbabwe Struggle: The Delayed Revolution Amagugu Publishers Bulawayo

Nhamo, A 2007 Immortalizing the Past: Reproduction of Zimbabwean Art by Lionnel Cripps Weaver Press Harare

Reynolds, P and Cousins, CC 1989 Lwaano Lwanyika: Tonga Book of Earth Panos Books London

Nyathi, P and Chikomo, K 2014a The Circle and Chevron Iconography in African Aesthetics: Celebrating the African Union's Golden Jubilee Amagugu Publishers Bulawayo

Nyathi, P and Chikomo K 2012 Zimbabwe's Traditional Dances: Woso Amagugu Publishers Bulawayo

Nyathi, P and Chikomo, K 2012 Zimbabwe's Traditional Dances: Jerusarema Mbende Amagugu Publishers Bulawayo

Nyathi, P and Chikomo, K 2015 Zimbabwe's Traditional Dances: Wosana Amagugu Publishers Bulawayo

Nyathi, P and Chikomo, K 2012 Understanding Arts and Culture in Schools Amagugu Publishers Bulawayo

Nyathi, P and Chikomo, K 2013 Understanding Arts and in Schools: Cultural Resource Centres   Amagugu Publishers Bulawayo

Nyathi, P nd Changing Material Culture of AmaNdebele Amagugu Publishers Bulawayo

Nyathi, P 2015 The History and Culture of the Babirwa of Botswana, South Africa and Zimbabwe Amagugu Publishers Bulawayo

Nyathi, P 2002 Traditional Ceremonies of AmaNdebele Mambo Press Gweru

Nzinga MuHera WavaNguni Ambuya MuHera 2015 The Way of the Light Book 2 Lutanga Shaba Harare

Pashapa, P 2009 Talking About Art Culture Fund of Zimbabwe Trust Harare

Pearson MP 2012 Exploring the Greatest Stone Age Mystery: Stonehenge Simon and Shuster London

Stewart, D 2005 Wisdom From Africa: A Collection of Proverbs Struik Lifestyle Cape Town

Stovel, H Stanley-Price, N and Killick, R Conservation of Living Religious Heritage-Papers From the ICCROM 2003 Forum on Living Religious Heritage: Conserving the Sacred ICCROM Rome

Printed in the United States
By Bookmasters